MODELS OF
MORAL EDUCATION
An Appraisal

MODELS OF MORAL EDUCATION

An Appraisal

Richard H. Hersh
John P. Miller
Glen D. Fielding

Longman Inc.

MODELS OF MORAL EDUCATION
An Appraisal

Longman Inc., New York
Associated companies, branches, and representatives
throughout the world.

Developmental Editor: Nicole Benevento
Interior Design: Pencils Portfolio, Inc.
Cover Design: Dan Serrano
Manufacturing and Production Supervisor: Louis Gaber
Composition: Book Composition Services
Printing and Binding: Fairfield Graphics Inc.

Manufactured in the United States of America

Library of Congress Cataloging in Publication Data

Hersh, Richard.
    Models of moral education.

    Includes bibliographical references and index.
    1. Moral education.   I. Miller, John, 1943–
joint author.   II. Fielding, Glen D., 1951–   joint
author.   III. Title.
LC268.H469   370.11′4   79-16409
ISBN 0-582-28123-7

9 8 7 6 5 4 3 2 1

CONTENTS

PREFACE

The public is demanding that schools become increasingly involved in moral education. More than two thirds of the respondents to 1975 and 1976 Gallup polls on education stated that schools should take on a share of the responsibility for the moral development of their students. The roots of this heightened interest in moral education are difficult to discover, but the 1954 U.S. Supreme Court decision in *Brown* v. *Topeka Board of Education*, which signaled a public debate on the morality of racism, may be a starting point. Since that time, the civil rights movement, the war on poverty, the Vietnam war, the women's movement, Watergate, and issues like abortion, corporate bribery, drug usage, ecology, homosexuality, and the rights of the handicapped have forced us to reconcile moral choices in a national public setting. Most recently, the suicide–mass murder of nine hundred persons in Jonestown, Guyana, has intensified the dilemma of balancing individual rights with social responsibility, a dilemma that has central significance in human development and institutional life.

Morality has also become a "media event" as television and film productions address serious moral questions. "Roots" and "Holocaust" broke television viewing records. Such exposure has greatly increased public awareness of the necessary moral dimension of human living. Awareness alone, however, is not sufficient. The moral questions remain unsolved, and the public seems to be asking schools to prepare future generations to provide more adequate answers. Yet, what the school's role should be in such an endeavor is unclear. Public debate concerning the nature of that role remains confused.

Professional educators are proposing a variety of means and ends of moral education. Many theories and models have been developed by philosophers, curriculum specialists, and psychologists. But, as often happens, either the creators or the followers of each approach to moral education espouse their viewpoints as if their particular model is sufficient to the task. Debates in public forums and in the professional literature often tend to reaffirm the belief that somewhere there is *the* answer to the moral education question. Yet the complexity of moral development causes us to believe that no one educational model, of those available at present, is sufficient. In writing this book, our major purpose is to demonstrate the need to see moral education as a combination of theories and models rather than rely on one model to the exclusion of others.

We have chosen for this demonstration six different models of moral education: rationale building, consideration, values clarification, value analysis, cognitive moral development, and social action. Other models exist, but these particular six represent theories most widely in use and contain materials associated with the models that have been among the most widely disseminated and most readily available. A major premise of this book is that the complexity of morality and moral development is such that educators must combine the strength of these models in order to do justice to the challenges of moral education in the schools. The beginning and ending chapters of this book emphasize this point.

Because moral education is such a complex endeavor, we have had to rely on a vast number of people for intellectual and moral support. Several of them merit specific mention. The concept for a compilation of models in book form originated in our work with the Ontario Institute for Studies in Education Moral Education Project in 1976. Clive Beck, Edmund Sullivan, John Eisenberg, and Dwight Boyd were faculty members associated with that project who helped force the recognition that no single model of moral education is sufficient to the task. Lawrence Kohlberg, both personally and through his writings, has modeled the quest for a wedding of theory and practice. Tom

Lickona has inspired our respect for hearing what teachers have to say on these matters.

Finally, we could not have completed this manuscript without the loving support and patience of Alison Baker, Jean Miller, and Marianne Hung. Special thanks are due Irene Glynn.

ACKNOWLEDGMENTS

We wish to thank the following for their kind permission to reprint illustrative materials used in this book:

For the quotations cited in chapter 3 and the example on pages 43–44: From Donald W. Oliver and James P. Shaver, *Teaching Public Issues in the High School.* Logan, Utah: Utah State University Press, 1974 (first published by Houghton Mifflin, 1966). Reprinted by permission of the author.

For the quotations cited in chapter 3 and the transcript on pages 40–42: From *Facing Value Decisions: Rationale-Building for Teachers* by James P. Shaver and William Strong. © 1976 by Wadsworth Publishing Company, Inc., Belmont, California 94002. Reprinted by permission of the publisher.

For the quotations cited in chapter 4 and the examples therein of the Lifeline program: From *Learning to Care,* by Peter McPhail, J.R. Ungoed-Thomas, and Hilary Chapman, © 1975 by The Schools Council and Longman Group Limited, London. Reprinted by permission of the publisher.

For the quotations cited in chapter 5 and the examples on pages 79–86, 88, and 93: From *Values and Teaching,* by Louis E. Raths, Merrill Harmin, and Sidney Simon, © 1978 by Charles E. Merrill Publishing Company, Columbus, Ohio. Reprinted by permission of the publisher.

For the adaptation by permission of the examples on pages 86–91: From *Values Clarification: A Handbook of Practical Strategies for Teachers and Students* by Sidney B. Simon, Leland W. Howe, and Howard Kirschenbaum. Copyright © 1972;

1

ISSUES IN MORAL EDUCATION

In an essay entitled "A Moral for an Age of Plenty," the scientist-philosopher Jacob Bronowski tells the story of Louis Slotin.[1] Slotin's tale reveals in dramatic form the common anatomy of morality, which all models of moral education seek to uncover.

Slotin was a nuclear physicist who worked in the laboratories at Los Alamos to help develop the atomic bomb. In 1946 he was conducting an experiment in the lab that required assembling pieces of plutonium. He was nudging one piece toward another, by tiny movements, in order to ensure that their total mass would be large enough to make a chain reaction, and he was doing it, as experts are prone to do such things, with a screwdriver. The screwdriver slipped, and the pieces of plutonium came a fraction too close together. Immediately, the instruments everyone was watching registered a great upsurge of neutrons, which was the sign that a chain reaction had begun. Radioactivity was filling the room.

"Slotin moved at once," Bronowski reports. "He pulled the pieces of plutonium apart with his bare hands. This was virtually an act of suicide, for it exposed him to the largest dose of radioactivity. Then he calmly asked his seven co-workers to mark their precise positions at the time of the accident in order that the degree of exposure of each one to the radioactivity could be fixed."

Having done this, and having alerted the medical service, Slotin apologized to his companions and said what turned out to be exactly true: he would die and they would recover.

In Slotin's response we see in heroic proportions what morality is ordinarily made of. We see, first, an uncompromising sense that other people matter, an unconditional concern for preserving individual life and welfare. We see, too, a finely honed ability to size up a situation impartially and accurately, a tested capacity for systematic thought. Finally, we witness the courage to act. Slotin did not merely feel compassion and think efficiently; he separated the plutonium.

Morality, as Slotin's case suggests, depends on the orchestration of humane caring, objective thinking, and determined action. Consider what would have happened in that lab if Slotin had expressed only one or two of these three faces of morality. If he had possessed the cool knowledge and quick intelligence of the scientist, but had felt nothing for his co-workers, how "moral" would his response have been? On the other hand, had he been unable to assess the problem rationally, how effective would his caring have been? And, however magnanimous his motives and logical his reasoning, what would they have amounted to if he had failed to act? Morality is neither good motives nor right reason nor resolute action; it is all three.

In Slotin's response the three elements of morality seemed to work as one. Indeed, there was no discernible separation between his feelings, thoughts, and action; they seemed to fit together at once, as part of a united front against a common threat. Yet, however entangled the individual strands of morality are in practice, there is a difference among them that is important to understand. For all the models of moral education treated in this book refer, directly or indirectly, to the separate processes of caring, judging, and acting. A general understanding of these three processes will thus help us see each of the model's individual perspectives in a clearer light.

CARING

Let us first consider the meaning of "caring." When we say that Slotin, for example, cared, what do we mean? We are implying, first, that he *wanted* to help, apart from any rational considerations. In this sense his caring was an unreflective "reaching out" to protect others. He felt impelled to assist his co-workers on a elemental emotional level. He was aroused to consider their interests. As a stimulus or motivation, caring seems to come from "the gut."

But, coupled with this state of emotional arousal, this active awakening of concern, we also imply by the term caring a certain level of social or psychological understanding. Had Slotin been unable to interpret the accident from the point of view of the other workers, he might not even have perceived that their lives were in danger, or that they might be saved. If he did not have the intellectual ability to assume the perspective of his fellows, how would he have known enough to feel concerned in the first place? Even feeling, then, calls upon an ability to know—to make inferences about people's needs and interests. To feel for another is to think of him as well. Can one imagine caring about a friend but being unable to show insight into the facts of his particular experience? To care about others is not only to want to consider their needs but to be able to do so. Caring thus involves both social motivation and social knowledge. As a moral educator, therefore, even if you emphasize the role of caring in morality (as, for example, McPhail's consideration model does), you are not doing exclusively "affective" education. For without the lens of thought, caring is blind. Learning to care about people is learning to know about them as well.

JUDGING

Caring, then, is not totally removed from reasoning, for without the ability to make inferences about another's needs, the motive to care wears thin, if it can be supported at all. Yet, in an important sense, reasoning is distinct from caring. Such is the case when we reason through, or judge, a moral problem, a problem in which the welfare of others is at stake. Certainly we must care about the parties involved in the decision or our reasoning will be empty or distorted. But even if we care deeply and understand clearly, the moral problem remains with us. Slotin, for instance, had to make a choice between competing moral claims: his life versus the lives of others. Caring about human life was not in itself sufficient to generate a solution to this dilemma. He still had to use his decision-making powers to reach a verdict. When we seek an answer to questions of moral obligation (i.e., those that ask us what our duty is in relation to a fellow human being), we engage in a process of deliberation. Should I tell my wife that I'm in love with my secretary? Should I fight in a war that seems unjust? Should I vote in favor of the referendum to support the new prison facilities? Conflicts such as these require more for their resolution than understanding the needs of others; they require the ability to make decisions among various shades of "good" and rival interpretations of the "right." The reasoning inherent in negotiating situations of moral conflict is thus more complex than the reasoning involved in caring. Moral judging depends upon caring, but goes beyond it in its intellectual demands.

While moral judgment is a complex business, in everyday discourse it sometimes seems as if moral decisions are more matters of simple opinion than considered thought. Students, for instance, often back their positions on controversial moral issues like abortion or euthanasia with comments such as these: "I just don't think it's right. Taking another person's life is morally wrong. That's my opinion, and I'm entitled to my opinion." These remarks are argument stoppers. The implication is that once one expresses a deep-seated opinion, further discussion is pointless. People will always have different opinions, so why press for rational justification?

Yet, as teachers, our tendency is to probe for reasons. "If you believe it wrong to take another's life," we might ask the student, "then would you kill in self-defense, or in the defense of your country?" If the student responds affirmatively to these questions, but still holds to the categorical statement that taking another's life is wrong, we conclude that his opinion is inadequately justified. To claim that an action is morally right or wrong is not simply to say that one prefers it in a particular situation; it is to suggest that the action is right in reference to a general standard of rightness. We cannot rest content with an appeal to mere opinion, as if a moral issue, such as the question of taking another's life, were a matter of personal taste. A person who says, "I think killing is wrong," is in effect saying, "You should think killing is wrong too, and I'll tell you why." Moral and value judgments imply reasons, and reasons, by their nature, cannot apply in a particular case only. If they apply in one case, they apply in all similar cases.[2] Moral judging, then, requires the ability to evaluate conflicting interests in the light of a consistent criterion, or principle.

ACTING

Perhaps the most important thing that can be said about action is that it is not moral or immoral in itself. Outside of a person's motives or judgments, his or her actions have no moral status. Slotin's separation of the plutonium was not moral per se. What made the act moral was the quality of caring and judging that guided it. It is true that we do at times seem to refer to certain acts as moral or immoral independent of their context. Murder, for instance, is universally condemned as immoral. But, at least in Western democracies, "murder" implies not merely the act of ending someone's life, but a malicious intent. Going to church every Sunday seems on the face of it a moral activity. But it's apparent that physical presence in a church says nothing about the moral character of the churchgoer. Specific habits, such as cleanliness, tidiness, or honesty, are often regarded as moral. These habits, however, do not carry built-in reasons for practicing them. That is, when we say that cleanliness is a moral habit, we normally mean by this that cleanliness promotes a more general good, such as personal health. In other words, specific behaviors may be said to be moral or immoral, but implicit in such pronouncements is an appeal to a further consideration, a motive or principle of right living.

But although we recognize that deeds or acts are not moral or immoral in themselves, as teachers we find it hard to avoid regarding certain behaviors as "right" and others as "wrong." When children hit one another, or cut in front of their classmates in line, or refuse to share materials, it certainly seems natural and appropriate to consider such behaviors as wrong and to stand firm against them. Similarly, when students cooperate with one another, volunteer to do clean-up work, or help others to understand new ideas, we don't hesitate to call such behavior "moral," even if the underlying motives and judgments of the students are left unexplored. In such cases we rely on common-sense generalizations about the relationship between certain outward behaviors and internal rational and emotional processes. When we see Susan hitting Bobby we intervene to stop it. We think it wrong even before probing the causes. Strictly speaking, hitting is not morally wrong in itself, for hitting could be done in self-defense or to ward off some grave danger, but common experience tells us that when children hit, their motives are less than magnanimous and their reasoning less than dispassionate. By the same token, if some of our students do volunteer work—reading literature to elderly blind people, for example—we tend to think that a highly "moral" pursuit. Of course, for all we know, the volunteers could be secretly planning to rob these people. The point is that we often accept certain deeds as moral or immoral on face value, in terms of circumstantial evidence, so to speak.

Moreover, as behavioral psychologists have suggested, it is probably necessary to reinforce basic "moral" behaviors, such as waiting one's turn, helping people in need, or sharing goods, even before children can fully fathom the rational justification for such behavior. Although, ultimately, children must come to appreciate the reasons behind their actions if they are to be morally responsible, the teacher cannot wait until the age of reason to enforce certain classroom rules and practices. As we shall see, the delicate art of moral education requires the teacher to promote habits of cooperation in her students and, at the same time, empower them to understand the logic of cooperation. Children must have practice in democratic living, to put the matter another way, in order to discover its intellectual justification on their own terms. Even though action is not a moral category per se, without opportunities for action, and reflection on action, it is difficult for moral development to take place. While teachers must be careful not to equate social conformity with morality, as nineteenth-century educators were prone to do, it may be that a firm grounding in convention provides an indispensable preparation on the route to moral autonomy. The goals of moral education must never be reduced to training in convention, but such training may be important in an auxiliary sense to the development of moral self-direction.

DEFINING AND SELECTING MODELS OF MORAL EDUCATION

A "model" of moral education, in our conception, is a way of thinking about the processes of caring, judging, and acting in an educational setting. A model includes a theory, or a point of view, about how people develop morally and a set of strategies, or principles, for fostering moral development. A model thus helps us both to understand and to practice moral education.

We have selected six models of moral education: rationale building, consideration, values clarification, value analysis, cognitive moral development, and social action. We have chosen these particular models for two reasons. First, each model has been used extensively, in one form or another, in the public schools. The rationale building approach has provided the intellectual power behind several major curriculum programs in the analysis of public issues (see the bibliography section of chapter 3 for specific references). The consideration model includes a three-part sequence of materials built around the theme of "learning to care." These materials have been field-tested by over twenty thousand students in Britain and have been recently adapted for an American audience. Values clarification is probably the most widely disseminated model. There are at least four handbooks of values clarification, replete with literally hundreds of exercises and techniques. Thousands of teachers have experimented with at least one version of values clarification. Although less universally popular than values clarification, value analysis, a systematic procedure for the resolution of value conflicts, has found favor among secondary social studies teachers. The cognitive developmental model, for its part, has formed the basis for scores of programs in moral development, from the Tacoma public school's interdisciplinary curriculum, "The Ethical Quest in a Democratic Society," to the *First Things: Values* curriculum published by Guidance Associates, to the "just community" school in Cambridge, Massachusetts (see chapter 7 for more complete references). Finally, the social action model reflects the theory and practice of those many community-oriented educational programs dedicated to building citizen effectiveness. This book focuses on these six models because they exemplify the main approaches to moral education currently in operation in the American public schools.

The models were chosen not only because they are representative but also because they are mutually complementary. Each model provides an essential part of the larger unity of moral education. While no single approach fully accounts for the processes of caring, judging, and acting, taken as a whole these six models go a long way toward creating such an account. The collective strengths of the models lay the foundation for a comprehensive program in moral education.

In the remainder of this chapter we introduce each model in terms of its special focus—the particular way it looks at the dimensions of caring, judging, and acting.

The Rationale Building Model

Although James Shaver's rationale building model casts light on all three aspects of morality, its primary concern is with the realm of judging. Shaver is more directly interested in teachers' moral decision making, however, than in students'. He seeks to help teachers understand the way values in general and moral values in particular affect decisions about instruction and classroom management. Shaver is especially sensitive to the pressures and risks that teachers face in confronting moral questions in the classroom. His model provides inspiration and guidance for teachers who wish to begin a moral education program. The rationale building scheme poses such basic questions as What is a value? What is a moral value? How do the values of a democratic society relate to the decisions teachers make in class? How, in a general sense, can teachers help their students develop more meaningful ways of dealing with moral issues? Shaver speaks to the core concerns of all models of moral education. It is thus fitting that we examine his model first.

The Consideration Model

The consideration model, created by Peter McPhail and his associates on the Schools Council Moral Education Curriculum Project of Great Britain, stresses the importance of caring, as distinct from judging. Part of McPhail's curriculum does deal with adjudicating moral conflicts, but the main focus is on learning to understand other people's needs rather than on balancing those needs as they conflict. According to McPhail, the task of moral education is to build on the fundamental core of consideration that all people naturally possess and "to demonstrate empirically that the differences among persons are superficial, while the similarities are profound." [3] The consideration model assumes that moral behavior is self-reinforcing, that "it is generally pleasant and rewarding to treat another considerately." [4] Whereas Shaver, and as we shall see, Kohlberg, argue that the student must encounter a certain measure of intellectual conflict to develop his or her moral potential, McPhail implies that the opportunity to express the sensitivity latent in all of us is most critical for moral development. The consideration approach thus places great emphasis on role playing, sociodrama, and creative writing as methods for enhancing interpersonal awareness.

Values Clarification

Values clarification sees moral education more in terms of promoting self-awareness and self-caring than in solving moral problems. The approach helps students discover and examine their values so as to achieve a more purposeful and secure sense of self. Judging is a key factor in the model, but it is a judging of what one likes and dislikes rather than of what one believes to be right or wrong. Values clarification does not accord moral values a special status within the range of values. All values, including moral ones, are considered personal and relative. Whereas each of the other models affirms that certain values, such as respect for human dignity, are more just and therefore more deserving of our commitment than other social values, values clarification sets forth no hierarchy of moral standards. The focus is on helping students get in touch with their present values rather than with helping them see their values in new ways.

Value Analysis

Value analysis helps students learn a highly systematic, step-by-step process for making moral decisions. Above all, the model is concerned with judging. Included in this framework are fine-tuned procedures for explaining distinctions between particular, general, and conditional facts, between value criteria and value principles, between relevant and irrelevant evidence, and between various tests of the acceptability of value principles. The model is most beneficial when coming to grips with complex policy issues. It helps students zero-in on specific components of the evaluative process before they get overwhelmed by the complexity of the whole. The value analysis methodology lends itself to moral questions that require social policy research. As such it is especially valuable to social studies educators. Nevertheless, with respect to the spheres of caring and acting, value analysis is silent.

The Cognitive Moral Development Model

The cognitive moral development model, like value analysis, is predominantly concerned with moral judgment. The overall aim of the approach is to help students think through moral controversy in increasingly clear and comprehensive ways. The purpose of engaging individuals in moral deliberation, from the cognitive developmental point of view, is not simply to teach specific information-processing and decision-making skills, as in value analysis. Rather, the purpose is to promote movement through general "stages" of moral judgment. As we will see in chapter 7, a stage is an organized system of thought, which underlies and gives direction to specific moral decisions. According to Lawrence Kohlberg, a professor of psychology and education at Harvard University and chief architect of the model, there are six stages of moral development through which all people progress (although as a result of environmental deficiencies, not everybody reaches the highest stages). Each stage offers a more comprehensive perspective on society and its relationship to individual rights. The research undertaken by Kohlberg and his colleagues suggests that movement through these stages can be promoted by engaging students in challenging moral decision making. Of particular value in facilitating stage advance is exposure to forms of reasoning one stage higher than that to which a student is accustomed. In the cognitive developmental model, learning to consider and respond to alternative points of view is not merely a matter of showing respect for one's classmates. It is an essential step toward developing a more advanced structure of moral reasoning. Although caring and acting find considerable expression in this framework, it should already be apparent that judging is the central concern.

The Social Action Model

More than any other approach, Fred Newmann's social action model, as the name implies, takes up the challenge of education for moral action. Newmann's model has been called the Ralph Nader version of moral education because it makes citizen action for change the main focus of the curriculum. Social action aims to increase students' effectiveness in uncovering, researching, and resolving social problems. Like Kohlberg, Newmann is concerned with developing students' moral reasoning. But Newmann gives more attention than does Kohlberg to the "environmental competencies" that sustain moral action. Newmann's point is that if students are not taught how to put their moral ideals into practice, their moral reflections and discussions will never get off the ground. How much interest will students show in deciding how society should change if they feel they are powerless to follow up on their decisions in practice? Learning how to exert influence in public affairs is a complex matter, and Newmann's program is long-term and inter-disciplinary. The model recommends both course work and community involvement. Newmann is careful, however, to distinguish his approach from "field study" or similar practicums in which students are simply turned loose in the community. The model articulates clear educational standards. It also frankly addresses its own limitations.

As a whole, the models furnish a broad-based pedagogy. Methods are presented to mobilize feeling, to guide thinking, and to sustain action. There are techniques designed to help students clarify personal interests, and there are methods that equip students to negotiate complex international problems. Considered collectively, we believe the models do justice to the complexity of moral education.

FORMAT OF THIS BOOK

In chapter 2 we present a short history of moral education in America that seeks to place the current interest in moral education in perspective. Chapters 3 through 8 present a summary of each model with an appraisal of its strengths and weaknesses, suggestions for using individual models enriched by contributions from one or more of the other models, as well as a bibliography of additional resource material. Chapter 9 ties the models together in terms of the themes of caring, judging, and acting. This last chapter makes the case for a broadly integrated approach to moral education, one that capitalizes on the strengths of all six models.

2
HISTORICAL CONTEXT FOR MORAL EDUCATION

Americans have always been concerned with the moral purposes of schooling. Throughout our history, the moral ends of education have inspired the most passionate rhetoric and the hottest debate. It is tempting to consider our present commitment to moral education as unique and new. But, for better or worse, moral education has always been with us, in one form or another.

Historically, Americans have linked their conception of moral education to the conditions of democracy. Particularly in the eighteenth and nineteenth centuries, moral education was embraced as the handmaiden of liberty, as a direct support of the democratic way of life. Although in recent years we have tended to view the connection between schooling and democracy in less direct, more subtle terms, moral education continues to be conceived and justified in the light of democratic principles.

Democracy places heavy demands on the moral capacities of the individual. It confronts each person with the need to choose among competing values and styles of life. It expects people to treat one another with decency without the pressure of external authority or fixed custom. It requires the individual to make informed judgments about personal interests and the welfare of the community. Not surprisingly, then, Americans have traditionally insisted that the success of democracy rests on the good character and right reason of the people. And, more often than not, the public has turned to the schools to promote, if not to guarantee, the moral competency of the next generation.

The notion of moral competency has been interpreted in many ways. Most commonly, it has been equated with respect for established institutions and conventions. In this sense, moral education has been a conservative force, aiming to take the risk out of democratic freedoms by assuring safe, "prosocial" behavior. During the early national period and continuing throughout most of the nineteenth century, the main purpose of moral education was to shape the child's habits in accordance with the stern virtues of the Puritan ethic: piety, loyalty, industry, and temperance. Moral education functioned as a narrow form of socialization.

In the late 1800s, habit formation was still the primary focus of moral education efforts, but the spartan virtues found themselves in competition with the gentler traits of expressiveness and benevolence. Moral education came to be seen as an affair of the heart. The child was still to be initiated into the rites of the status quo, but the methods of persuasion were to be more tender. Rather than appealing to children's fears of eternal damnation or financial ruin, the "romantic" approach to moral education capitalized on children's natural sentiments. Democracy was to be preserved through bonds of affection.

Educational progressivism, a reform movement that began around the turn of the twentieth century, went beyond the romantic preoccupation with the immediate feelings of the child and the Puritan insistence on obedience to create a new vision of democratic schooling. John Dewey, the quintessential progressive philosopher, argued that democracy was a fluid process, a moving constellation of people constructing and reconstructing their own values and meanings in the light of their changing situations. Morality, too, Dewey maintained, was a dynamic process of social problem solving rather than a set of inert ideas or habits. Moral education, in the progressive framework, was to serve democracy, but a democracy sustained by the creative and critical capacities of the individual and not merely by hard work or good nature. While progressivism suffered a near-fatal setback in the 1950s, an updated and fortified conception of progressivism made its way back into the schools in the mid-1960s. Indeed, taken as a whole, the models presented in this book reflect a reaffirmation of the progressive philosophy. While the models go beyond Dewey's formulation in their more finely tuned psychological support and their more elaborated teaching strategies, the progressive faith in group activity and discussion, and in rational deliberation, is clear.

When the Founding Fathers spoke of education, they rarely missed the chance to point out its moral mission. The call of the schools, it was widely acknowledged, was to prepare people for the responsibilities of freedom. Such preparation required a highly deliberate program in religious and moral instruction, for without piety and virtue "no people ever continued, for a long time, either respectable, happy, or free." [1] Education for democracy was directed toward the development of Protestant rectitude, as well as secular erudition. Moral and spiritual training were considered indispensable requirements of democracy:

The enjoyment of liberty is not for all at all times. It is an instrument too delicate for a clumsy performer; it is safe only in the masterhand. To distinguish between the boundaries of rational liberty and mad licentiousness requires a temperament of soul and a perpetuation of sentiment which they only possess who have long considered the question and rendered the subject familiar. [2]

It is highly important that every order and class of citizens exert themselves in the cultivation of those sentiments and principles on which rest our political happiness and national existence. Knowledge and religion are the supports of a republican government. The means of education, and moral and religious instruction, ought therefore to engage our serious and vigorous attention. [3]

In the early years of the Republic, the teacher's role as moral educator was to train her charges in the habits of piety and obedience. Any hint of irreverence or rebelliousness on the part of students seemed to pose a threat to the fragile unity of the infant nation. In the Boston public schools, the first public system in the country, each of the readers used for spelling, grammar, and composition (*The Boston Primer, Child's Companion,* and *Beauties of the Bible,* for example) attempted to instill in students a sense of religious duty and deference to authority. In the *Boston Primer* of 1808 the teaching of reading and morals was combined in materials like the following:

> Let Children who would fear the LORD, •
>   Hear what their Teachers fay,
>
> With rev'rence meet their Parents' word,
>   And with Delight obey.

In Adam's Fall	A Dog will bite
We finned All.	A Thief at Night.
Thy Life to mend.	The Eagle's Flight
God's book attend.	Is out of Sight.
The Cat doth play,	The idle Fool
And after flay.	Is whipt at School.[4]

As is apparent from the *Primer,* God was ever present in the early-nineteenth-century schoolhouse. And, as Carl Kaestle has noted, "although He was said to be nondenominational, He acted distinctively like a Puritan." [5] Moral education was in essence a form of religious instruction during this era. People thought of social problems in moral terms, and "almost no one could think of morals as separate from God and the Bible." [6]

One means of moral training, in the New York City public schools at least, was straightforward catechism, as in this persuasive charge recited by teacher and students:

T: You must obey your parents.
S: I must obey my parents. [The pupils, at each repetition, place the right hand, opened, upon the breast.]
T: You must obey your teachers.
S: I must obey my teachers.[7]

The litany continued, Kaestle reports, with injunctions against lying, stealing, and swearing. Then, "slowly and in a soft tone,"

T: God always sees you.
S: God always sees me.
T: God hears all you say.
S: God hears all I say.
T: God knows all you do.
S: God knows all I do.[8]

Perhaps an even more powerful sanction for moral behavior were the rules of the school. Children were required to be courteous, obedient, punctual, clean, and faithful in attendance. As an enforcement technique, it was common practice to enlist student leaders in the task of proclaiming around the school the names of students expelled on account of their bad conduct.[9] Needless to say, this practice exploited peer pressure with a vengeance.

However efficient these traditional modes of moral education seemed, they were put to a severe test in the latter half of the nineteenth century as the composition of the student population changed markedly. Increasingly, teachers confronted children of foreign birth or immigrant parents, working-class students who spent more time in the factory and tenement than on the farm or in church. Society was growing more pluralistic, more secular, and more volatile. No longer was there a guarantee that the values children learned in the home would reinforce those taught in the school. Parents themselves were now part of the problem, for many of them came from strange places like Italy, Hungary, and Russia whose customs and beliefs seemed to defy the conventions of Protestant America. The swelling body of immigrant working-class youth, concentrated in the nation's cities, alarmed laymen and educators alike. These unschooled masses seemed easy prey to the doctrines of socialism and anarchism. The fears of social and political breakdown, which recalled the fears of the early republicans for the nation's survival, could be allayed, or so it seemed to many, only through the agency of the school. The school stood as the ultimate bulwark against crime, revolution, and degeneracy. Only with the laboring and immigrant young safely in class, it was decided, would prosperity continue and freedom survive.

Moral education in the late nineteenth century became an effort to "redeem" immigrant and working-class children from the influences of their family background. Moral education was the curricular counterpart of the "melting pot." The school's mission was to civilize and "Americanize" the strangers in the land. In the words of one state board of education:

> The danger to civilization is not from without, but from within. The heterogeneous masses must be made homogeneous. Those who inherit the traditions of other and hostile nations; those who are bred under diverse influences and hold foreign ideas; those who are supported by national inspirations not American must be assimilated and Americanized. The chief agency to this end has been the public school and popular education. No better agency has ever been devised by man.[10]

Moral education was thus interpreted as a narrow and unreflective form of socialization. Students were to be digested into the common life and processed in a single direction. The traditional virtues of piety and obedience, however secularized in form, continued to be imposed on a new generation of students.

This "hard-nosed," fear-infused perspective on moral education, while a powerful force in educational circles, did not go unchallenged. Toward the end of the century, a host of "child-centered" pedagogues, armed with new theories of child development, began to suggest that the hope for democracy lay not in indoctrination but in love. Teachers needed to show concern for the particular needs of the child, especially those needs relating to emotional self-expression and activity. Gentle nurturance and affection would assure good habits.

Kate Wiggin's *Children's Rights*, published in 1892, was a popular statement of the hope of building moral character without depriving the child of the pleasures of childhood. Mrs. Wiggin warned the parent and the teacher that children should not be forced to be "too good," against their natures. Intellectual and moral development might constrict the growth of character. Wiggin stressed the value of teaching by example rather than by drill or lecture. She argued that most children "have a tolerably clear sense of right and wrong needing only gentle guidance to choose the right when it is put before them." [11] They have "a natural sense of what is true and good" and will choose what is good if it is made understandable and attractive. The job was to "provide the conditions of mental growth and then let the child do the growing." [12] For Wiggin, as for many of the more optimistic educators of the day, the child was naturally good. Moral education was more a matter of nurturance than instruction.

Undoubtedly the most influential of the early child-centered educators was G. Stanley Hall. During the 1890s Hall, who had earned Harvard's first doctorate in psychology and had assumed the first presidency of Clark University, rose to prominence as one of the foremost figures in American psychology and education. Like Wiggin, Hall had great faith in the natural potential of the child. In Hall's view, the greatest service the teacher could perform in the formation of moral character was to avoid interfering in the child's growth:

> The guardians of the young should strive first of all to keep out of nature's way, and to prevent harm, and should merit the proud title of defenders of the happiness and rights of children. They should feel profoundly that childhood, as it comes fresh from the hands of God, is not corrupt, but illustrates the survival of the most consummate thing in the world; they should be convinced that there is nothing else so worthy of love, reverence, and service as the body and soul of the growing child. [13]

As Hall conceived it, naturalism in education was an aggressively nonintellectual, if not antiintellectual, doctrine. [14] Emotional force was elevated over critical judgment. Academic training was to give ground to "health, growth, and heredity, a pound of which is worth a ton of instruction." [15] Hall's approach to moral education was designed to produce contented and vigorous people, but not necessarily free and responsible ones. Hall was, in fact, an elitist and reactionary, however liberating his child-centered rhetoric might have seemed. For Hall was convinced that only the genetically gifted could benefit from intellectual education and that the main purpose of education was to train good parents, efficient workers, and loyal citizens. [16] Like most Americans, Hall believed that education was the foundation of democracy. But his vision of democracy was racist and childlike. Although not all the romantic approaches to moral education glorified juvenile idealism to the extent that Hall's did, as the champion of the movement Hall can hardly be dismissed as an isolated eccentric. His application of "naturalism" to education reached a wide audience.

The naturalistic approach to moral instruction was thus as conservative in purpose as the more mechanical method of character training stemming from the Puritan tradition. Both approaches were intended to perpetuate the cultural values of secularized Protestantism. Whether thrown callously into the cultural melting pot or bathed warmly in the sentiments of the middle class, the outcome was to be much the same: the child would be adjusted to the terms of convention. Moral education was merely an instrument for inducting students into the established order.

Looming within the educational landscape of the 1890s, however, was the reform movement known as progressivism. Progressivism took many forms, but its impact in moral education was most clearly felt in the area of ideology. In the works of the philosopher John Dewey, the progressive conception of moral education emerged as a potent rival to the Puritan and romantic formulations.

Dewey envisioned a diverse society held together by a common commitment to the use of intelligence in the solution of human problems. Education would help provide social cohesion, not by drilling children in specific moral rules or by showing them examples of "nice" behavior, but by developing intellectual power. Moral education, according to Dewey, centered in reflective thought, not in character training or heart warming. Academic, or intellectual, education in turn was itself moral education in that, when done properly, it addressed problems of direct personal and social significance to the student. Moral and intellectual education were essentially two sides of the same coin because both aimed to promote the use of reason, or the scientific method, in human affairs:

Our conceptions of the ethical in education have been too narrow, too formal, and too pathological. We have associated the term ethical with certain special acts which are labelled virtues and set off from the mass of other acts, and still more from the habitual images and motives in the agents performing them. Moral instruction is thus associated with teaching about these particular virtues, or with instilling certain sentiments in regard to them. The ethical has been conceived in too goody-goody a way. But it is not such ethical ideas and motives as these which keep men at work in recognizing and performing their moral duty. Such teaching as this, after all is said and done, is external; it does not reach down into the depths of the character-making agency. Ultimate moral motives and forces are nothing more nor less than social intelligence—the power of observing and comprehending social institutions—and social power—trained capacities of control—at work in the service of social interest and aims. There is no fact which throws light upon the constitution of society, there is no power whose training adds to social resourcefulness which is not ethical in its bearing.[17]

Dewey's treatment of moral education was not confined to an analysis of classroom instruction. For Dewey recognized that the "hidden curriculum," the unstated goals and messages of schooling, were in many cases more powerful influences on the child's moral development than the formal curriculum. In Dewey's view, children learned moral values from the quality of their total social experience. They learned about the workings of democracy, for example, through participating in and reflecting on democratic processes. If the schools did not provide the experience of democracy, no amount of formal academic study could ever communicate its meaning. In traditional schools, the ethical principles of democracy were conveyed as remote abstractions, just as subject matter was prescribed as a bitter pill to swallow. According to Dewey, intellectual and ethical competence could be achieved only by reflecting on one's actual, concrete experience. Even if the teacher introduced concepts like democracy, justice, respect for others, and human rights, if the classroom and school structure continued to model and enforce authoritarian social relations, no effective learning would take place. This concern with relating abstractions to the child's own experience was Dewey's understanding of "child-centeredness." Children needed to live the moral ideals they were expected to master intellectually.

The experiential base of moral education in Dewey's framework was cooperative group activity. Working with others on actual problems, in whatever field—art, science, politics, mechanics—helped the student appreciate the perspective of others and the value of mutual exchange. Morality could not be taught merely by the teacher's example or word. Students needed to interact with one another on projects that were of real concern to them:

> Upon the ethical side, the tragic weakness of the present school is that it endeavors to prepare future members of the social order in a medium in which the conditions of the social spirit are eminently wanting. . . .
> Where the school work consists in simply learning lessons, mutual assistance, instead of being the most natural form of cooperation and association, becomes a clandestine effort to relieve one's neighbor of his proper duties. Where active work is going on, all this is changed. Helping others, instead of being a form of charity which impoverishes the recipient, is simply an aid in setting free the powers and furthering the impulse of the one helped. A spirit of free communication, of interchange of ideas, suggestions, results, both successes and failures of previous experiences, becomes the dominating note of the recitation . . . if the end in view is the development of a spirit of social cooperation and community life, discipline must grow out of and be relative to this. . . . That we learn from experience, and from books or the sayings of others only as they are related to experience, are not mere phrases. . . . [A social spirit] only comes from having a part to do in constructive work.[18]

The influence of Dewey's conception of moral education was most visible in the period between the two world wars. In many secondary schools, open-ended discussion of controversial social issues, stimulated by contemporary films and magazines, became standard fare, and numerous community-involvement projects were initiated. Students and teachers alike tended to be more active and less formal in their relationship with each other.[19] The stress on group exploration of ongoing social problems gave rise, moreover, to such architectural innovations as laboratories, shops, movable furniture and partitions, assembly rooms, and kitchens. On the eve of the Second World War, Dewey's dynamic theory of moral education seemed to hold sway over all others.

By the mid-1950s, however, the progressive educational movement had all but died. For progressivism had become, in

Lawrence Cremin's terms, "a complex pedagogical mystique, mastered by the initiates but virtually incomprehensible to laymen concerned with the making of educational policy." [20] Dewey's notion of linking the life of the classroom to the world of the community was grossly misinterpreted to mean adjusting the child to the status quo. His commitment to the development of creative intelligence was all but forgotten as educators became preoccupied with group experience as an end in itself. Whereas Dewey saw cooperative activity as a springboard for critical reflection, many teachers elevated activity itself as the aim of education. Progressive schools were pilloried during the 1950s as "time-wasters," educational "wastelands," and "playhouses"; and title like "Lollipops v. Learning," and "Treason in the Textbooks" appeared with increasing regularity in the contemporary journals. [21]

The 1950s were an inhospitable time for moral education, or for any form of study that smacked of "progressivism." The nation was preoccupied with expanding its economic and military might. Moral education took a back seat to technical and academic training. Particularly after the Russian's successful launching of the satellite *Sputnik I,* the clamor for high-quality education in science, math, and foreign languages became strident. If the nation expected to compete effectively with the Soviet Union, on either the economic or military front, the schools, so popular wisdom held, had to spend less time on "soft" areas like moral education and more time on academic staples. Democracy seemed to hinge less on the moral autonomy of the individual than on the size of the gross national product and the quantity of nuclear warheads.

But by the late 1960s, the drive for accelerated intellectual and technical training had reached an impasse, and the need for moral education asserted itself anew. Protests over Vietnam, demands for civil rights, riots in the cities, and campus shutdowns drowned out the cry for mastery of the traditional disciplines. Social justice, in the schools as well as in society at large, seemed a much more crucial concern than technological sophistication. America's economic prosperity, critics insisted, belied a deep-rooted moral bankruptcy. Poverty, racism, imperialism, and sexism could no longer be swept neatly under the class-room rug. Indeed, schools seemed as much part of the problem as the solution. American education was indicted for instilling in children the "fear of failure," and "the nightmare of defeat." Schools were accused of valuing competition over cooperation and subservience over independence. They were portrayed as efficient custodial institutions, not unlike mental hospitals and prisons, where children learned to cope with the mechanical routines and dehumanizing rituals of mass society. The educational system appeared as a vast sorting machine that sifted the privileged from the disadvantaged and maintained the stratified order of an unjust capitalist society.[22]

Moral education now became tied to a broad-based movement for social justice. As Jerome Bruner, a leading educational psychologist, suggested, justice was taken as both a condition and an end of education:

> In the end, we must finally appreciate that education is not a neutral subject, nor is it an isolated subject. It is a deeply political issue in which we guarantee a future for someone and, frequently, in guaranteeing a future for someone, we deal somebody else out. If I had my choice now, in terms of a curriculum project for the seventies, it would be to find a means whereby we could bring society back to its sense of values and priorities in life. I believe I would be quite satisfied to declare, if not a moratorium, then something of a deemphasis on matters that have to do with the structure of history, the structure of physics, the nature of mathematical consistency, and deal with it rather in the context of the problems that face us. We might better concern ourselves with how those problems can be solved, not just by practical action, but by putting knowledge, wherever we find it, to work in these massive tasks. We might put vocation and intention back into the process of education, much more firmly than we had it there before.[23]

Bruner's plea for restoring to education its social and moral meaning struck a responsive chord in a nation torn by political dissent and cultural alienation. To make the ideal of justice a living concern to students seemed a pressing educational priority. It is thus more than a historical coincidence that each of the models of moral education discussed in this book was born during this period, the late 1960s and early '70s. For the models, taken as a whole, are concerned with helping students bring to light the moral complexities of democratic living, not only as they appear in the corridors of Congress but in the rules and roles of the school as well. Unlike nineteenth-century approaches, these models do not propose to take the risks out of democracy, but to make those risks more intelligible. Like the progressive conception, of which they are descendants, the models emphasize the reciprocal relationship between the theory and practice of justice. Students must have actual experience in moral decision making if they are to come to understand the meaning of moral principles. Unlike the traditional faith in the power of moral education to safeguard, or to perfect, democracy, these models are cautious in their assessments of the impact of their programs. Moral education is not portrayed as a salvation for our times. It emerges less as a way out of the problems of democracy than as a way of handling problems more effectively.

The American educator has always been a moral educator. Whether from the austere Puritan or the indulgent romantic, children have traditionally received moral training. What is new about current perspectives on moral education is not their explicit concern for morality but their awareness of moral complexity. In the tradition of John Dewey, the models presented here affirm the importance of long-term experience and systematic reflection, of a social spirit and a moral imagination, of formal reasoning and creative caring. If moral education is more complex and challenging in the 1980s than in the past, it is not because morality has become more important. It is because we can no longer afford to treat morality in one-dimensional terms. As the rights and responsibilities of democratic living become more complex, so too must our efforts in moral education.

3
THE RATIONALE BUILDING MODEL

James Shaver's rationale building model addresses the teacher as philosopher rather than as strategist. Shaver aims to help teachers build an explicit rationale for teaching value-laden issues. His fundamental purpose is to sharpen teachers' understanding of the moral basis of teaching; only indirectly is he concerned with developing teaching techniques and curricula.

Shaver's model suggests ways of thinking about values and moral education; it does not make methodological prescriptions. Nonetheless, the approach contains pedagogical implications. The methodology linked most directly with Shaver's conceptual frame is the "jurisprudential model" for the teaching of public issues, a model Shaver helped create and articulate in the early 1960s. The jurisprudential model focused exclusively on social studies education. Shaver's more recent concern has been to enlarge upon the original jurisprudential scheme and extend its explanatory power to other areas of value-related education.

Shaver views moral education primarily from the perspective of a democratic and pluralistic society. Like the cognitive moral development model and value analysis, the rationale building approach emphasizes the role of critical reflection, on the part of teachers and students alike, in moral education. But whereas Kohlberg is mainly concerned with developing students' general structure of moral reasoning, Shaver focuses on the need to teach the specific analytic skills he deems essential to democratic citizenship. And whereas value analysis concentrates on elaborating and exemplifying a hierarchy of such skills, Shaver devotes more attention to exploring the democratic tradition from which the skills are derived. Shaver's main purpose is to place moral education in a broad social context.

THEORY

In large measure, the theoretical framework of Shaver's model is the model itself. As developed in *Facing Value Decisions: Rationale-building for Teachers*,[1] which Shaver co-authored with William Strong, the theoretical base consists of three parts: (1) a definition of values, (2) the nature of democracy, and (3) an analysis of moral education in a democratic society.

A Definition of Values

In Shaver's terms, values are "standards and principles for judging worth. They are the criteria by which we judge 'things' (people, objects, ideas, actions, and situations) to be good, worthwhile, desirable; or, on the other hand, bad, worthless, despicable; or, of course, somewhere in between these extremes. We may apply our values consciously. Or they may function unconsciously, as part of the influence of our frames of reference, without our being aware of the standards implied by our decisions."[2]

This definition contains three key elements. The first is that values are concepts, not feelings. Values embody and express feelings, Shaver emphasizes, but they are more than feelings. They are standards of judgment with rational content. Because of this rational content, values can be defined, analyzed, and compared with other values. For example, responsibility is a value by which we often judge the actions of ourselves and others. The idea of responsibility no doubt calls forth a positive emotional reaction, and we may experience negative feelings toward people or actions that we consider irresponsible. But the value of responsibility is not just a vague feeling of approval or disapproval. It is a concept that carries criteria for rating behaviors as responsible, irresponsible, or some degree in between. Values thus hold affect, but their defining structure is cognitive.

The second key element in the definition is that values exist in the mind independently of self-awareness or public affirmation. In Shaver's theory, a value does not have to be explicitly announced or put into practice to qualify as a value. A value may be held tacitly. Shaver is here distinguishing his definition of value from that offered in the values clarification scheme (see chapter 5). Whereas values clarification recognizes as values only those beliefs that have been chosen rationally and acted on repeatedly, Shaver argues that certain values operate beneath the surface of rational choice and overt action. For example, a man may value hard work even though he never made an explicit choice to work hard or openly declared his commitment to it. Perhaps he always worked hard out of economic necessity. At the same time, he may judge the worth of other people in terms of how hard they work. Even if the fellow never comes right out and says that hard work is important to him, Shaver would argue that such work is a value to him nonetheless. Values often form a part of our frame of judgment without our conscious knowledge or deliberate choosing.

The third element in Shaver's definition is that values are dimensional rather than absolute categories. That is, they are criteria for judging degrees of good and bad, right and wrong, or praise and blame; they are not simply the presence or absence of these characteristics. Take the examples of hard work and responsibility. These are surely not all-or-nothing categories. We seldom consider a person to be totally responsible or completely lazy. People's behavior falls along a continuum of responsibility-irresponsibility or hardworking-lazy. Values are sets of rules for rating behavior or objects along a continuum of worth.

Shaver distinguishes between values and value judgments. Value judgments are the assertions we make on the basis of our values. Values are grounds, not conclusions. To cite one of Shaver's examples, a teacher who says, "Duke, you should get to class on time," is making a value judgment. The value, or criterion, which supports that judgment may be punctuality, or classroom or social order, or respect for institutional authority. In any case, values are constructs that underlie value judgments, not judgments per se.

If we are to act with consistency, Shaver maintains, we must try to make explicit the relationship between our value judgments and our values. Value judgments cannot justify themselves; to assess their appropriateness and propriety we must consult the values (as well, of course, as the relevant facts) on which they are based. Thus, a value need not be understood consciously to qualify as a value, but the effort to bring to light our values is nonetheless worth the effort. For it is much easier to act in terms of one's values when one knows what they are. A teacher who is fully aware that he values independence of thought, for example, will surely make a more deliberate attempt to reinforce original responses in class than he would if this value remains hidden. In stressing the importance of being aware of one's values and acting on them consistently, Shaver reveals an affinity with the authors of values clarification, who make value awareness a central feature of their model.

Unlike values clarification, however, Shaver's model invites us to examine values not only in relation to specific judgments or actions but in relation to other values. Values need to be understood as interlocking parts of a total value network, rather than as self-contained units. Because our values are linked to one another, one value often impinges on another. For example, we may value both liberty and equality. The value of liberty directs us to maximize individual freedom and self-expression. The value of equality guides us to guarantee each individual the same access to public goods. Yet, in fulfilling the claims of equality, we often compromise the ideal of liberty. We may believe, say, that the wealthy should pay progressively more taxes than the poor, even if the wealthy claim that this restricts their economic freedom. Or, we may believe that minority groups should be given preferential treatment in hiring so that they will have an equal chance for success, even though this may limit the liberty of nonminorities to secure positions. The point is not so much whether we value liberty or equality, but how we balance these values when they conflict in concrete situations of choice. Being aware of our values is not enough, Shaver argues. We must explore how our values affect one another.

Shaver points out that it is often tempting to segregate one set of values from another. For example, in the business world we may act on the belief that a man who fails has no one to blame but himself. At church, however, we affirm that people ought to be charitable in assisting those who are less fortunate. Thomas Green, an educational philosopher, lends eloquent support to Shaver's contention:

> It is possible to hold conflicting sets of beliefs as psychologically central because we tend to order our beliefs in little clusters encrusted about, as it were, with a protective shield that prevents any cross fertilization among them or any confrontation between them. Thus, one may praise the value of competition as an article of economic faith and support, at the same time, the necessity for cooperation as a fundamental demand of social ethics. In this way, we can simultaneously hold to certain core beliefs which are at many points logically incompatible. This is perfectly possible, as long as we never permit our cluster of economic beliefs to influence our ethical convictions or permit our ethical beliefs to touch our economic thought. The protective shield by which we guarantee such a segregation of beliefs usually appears disguised as a belief itself. We say "Ethics has nothing to do with the necessities of business," or "Religion ought to stay out of politics." A student, for example, may possess a religious faith that militates against the demands of inquiry. He may be a successful student, nonetheless, provided he never permits his religious faith to influence his understanding of his studies.[3]

Although it is common to try to isolate one "cluster" of values from another, a fundamental goal of moral education, or any education for that matter, is to help students see their personal values as a whole. In Shaver's view, among the three most important categories of values that enter into the activity of teaching are aesthetic values, instrumental values, and moral values. Understanding how these value categories fit together is a basic task for the moral educator and, ultimately, for students as well.

Aesthetic values are those standards by which we judge beauty. Teachers of the humanities consider the aesthetic dimensions of their subject more directly than do other teachers, yet we often hear math teachers speak of the "elegance" of a formal proof, or physical education instructors comment on the grace and beauty of a physical performance. Everyone makes aesthetic judgments, even if only to appraise someone's personal appearance.

Shaver stresses that aesthetic judgments are distinct from moral judgments. When we confuse aesthetic propositions with attributions of virtue or morality, we seriously distort their meaning. To say that a student's dirty hair is unattractive, or aesthetically displeasing, is not to say that the student is immoral, in spite of suggestions that may be made to this effect by some principals and parents.

Shaver makes a point of distinguishing not only between aesthetic and moral values but between moral and instrumental values. Instrumental values are standards set in order to achieve other standards. They are derivative rather than fundamental principles. For example, in teaching, many of our standards of classroom management are instrumental values. Rules concerning discipline, attentiveness, and punctuality are upheld, presumably, not as ends in themselves but as means toward effective learning. Dress codes are generally justified on the grounds that highly idiosyncratic styles of dress interfere with the learning atmosphere of the school and are inimical to the education of all students. Specific instructional objectives often embody instrumental values in relation to more general and long-term educational goals. Instrumental values are intermediary standards designed to serve larger ends.

We need to guard against confusing instrumental and moral values, Shaver cautions. Just as teachers may be offended by students who do not share their tastes in music or personal dress, so they may consider students "bad" or even "immoral" if they talk out of turn in class. Teachers need to resist the tendency to moralize about instrumental values.

Moral values, in Shaver's terminology, are "the standards, the principles, by which we judge whether aims or actions are proper." [4] Two features of moral values are stressed: (1) they vary widely in their importance and applicability, and (2) they are more than merely matters of personal taste.

Shaver places moral values along a continuum from personal preferences to basic values. Thus, such values as solitude and cleanliness would constitute the least significant moral values because they mainly involve issues of personal preference. The value of the sanctity of human life, on the other hand, would be considered the most basic value because it is essential to our humanity. In a democratic society, basic values include the principles of freedom of speech, equal protection of the law, and religious freedom.

Between the poles of personal preference and basic values lie a wide range of "middle-level" moral values. Honesty, cooperation, and patriotism qualify as middle-level values. They are not grounded in human nature, yet they are important social conventions.

While moral values may differ in their degree of importance and generality, all moral values express something more than a purely individual standard. "Because moral values are used to justify and judge ethical decisions, and these have impact on other people, moral standards are not merely matters of personal taste." [5] When we are faced with a moral decision (i.e., a decision that affects the welfare of others), we need to ask what we *ought* to do, rather than what we might like to do. Deciding whether abortion, or capital punishment, or euthanasia is right or wrong is simply not on the same level with deciding whether or not to have an extra helping of mashed potatoes for dinner. Unlike aesthetic or instrumental values, moral values necessarily carry a basic message of obligation.

Understanding the differences between aesthetic, instrumental, and moral values is not merely an academic exercise, Shaver makes clear. Conflicts between these classes of value, and within each class, are unavoidable. Handling value conflicts effectively demands insight into the meaning and function of one's values. As we shall see later in this chapter, teaching students to negotiate value conflicts is a crucial element in Shaver's framework.

The Nature of Democracy

The basic moral value that undergirds and sustains a democracy is the principle of individual dignity. The concept of dignity holds that to be human is in itself important and demands respect. Each person has intrinsic or inherent worth. The individual deserves consideration by virtue of his or her humanness, apart from considerations of wealth, race, sex, or physical or intellectual ability.

One of the defining attributes of the ideal of dignity is the right to make important choices. Our essential human nature requires that we be able to exercise the freedom of self-determination, that we can create our own life plan. The right to choose is the right to shape one's reality and not merely be shaped by it.

Another essential characteristic of the ideal of dignity is the belief in intelligence, or reason. The faith in intelligence supports the notion of free choice. It suggests that each individual has the potential for making wise and just choices because he or she possesses reason. To judge a problem rationally is to take all relevant facts and interests into account and evaluate them from a disinterested perspective—a perspective understandable to all who are competent to investigate the issue. Intelligence enables an individual to survey and assess comprehensively the possibilities of choice. Because humans are rational beings, we trust in their potential for autonomous decision making.

The right to make important decisions is given meaning only within the conditions of pluralism. Without a variety of openly expressed views, values, and styles, the ideal of freedom of choice is a hollow abstraction, and the facility for making rational judgments cannot be exercised. The presence of a multiplicity of political, professional, and cultural groups generates and sustains the alternative ways of life that make fundamental choice possible. In a monolithic society, there are few alternatives and few choices. The individual's freedom of self-determination is constricted. The cultural materials with which the individual fashions an identity are plain and uniform. Pluralism widens the range of choice. It lends texture, color, and dimension to one's alternatives. Pluralism is an indispensable condition for democracy, for it is the only natural mechanism that can guarantee meaningful freedom of choice.

Pluralism not only makes authentic choice possible but it promotes critical and reasoned judgment. The pressure of diverse views in the community encourages open-mindedness. In many situations, latent problems that may be overlooked by people with similar outlooks on life can be uncovered by less conventional individuals. Shaver gives an example of a newcomer to a neighborhood questioning the treatment of minority groups in a community that "has no minority problem." The resultant consternation may be unwelcome, but it often activates the decision-making process. Moreover, once the problem is presented, diversity of opinion can provide a broad range of options from which to work out solutions. Value conflict in society is potentially constructive.

Pluralism, then, promotes the use of reason, as well as providing the conditions of choice. It is a cornerstone of democracy. But meaningful pluralism depends on more than the existence of a variety of groups. Individuals need a common framework in which to relate, an underlying agreement on basic norms of communication and fairness. If pluralism is to go beyond the clash of competing interests, a certain level of social cohesion and consensus is necessary. For democracy to function, people must share a basic allegiance to the democratic ethic. They must believe in the dignity of the individual and the value of reason and truth. Diversity can flourish only within a context of unity.

National unity rests ultimately on a common faith in fundamental democratic values. On a more immediate and concrete level, unity is built on respect for the relatively specific procedures established for the regulation of interpersonal and intergroup conflict. Principles like dignity and rationality are too vague to be useful as normative criteria for mediating social conflicts. They must be translated into values with more concrete meaning, such as the principles of freedom of speech, press, and religion, or the doctrines of equal protection of the law and "one man, one vote." More recently institutionalized democratic values are the right to decent shelter, adequate food, and equal educational opportunity. Such basic moral standards are also instrumental values, for they serve the overarching end of human dignity.

In Shaver's view, there is an "American creed" that carries a common emotional meaning. On the affective level, people are committed to the standard of dignity and its derivative values and procedures. A unifying democratic faith exists. But the consensus is general and emotional, not a consensus on the level of rational interpretation or application. The "descriptive" or cognitive meaning of basic values is often in serious dispute. When a value like equality of educational opportunity is applied to a specific situation or policy—for example, should inner city blacks be bused into suburban schools?—the descriptive meaning of the term must be explicated. Otherwise it is impossible to determine rationally whether the policy in question satisfies or violates the value criterion. As descriptive meaning is specified, people may construe a value term differently because of their different experiences and, consequently, different frames of reference, and conflict may result. People may share a reverence for fundamental democratic norms but disagree on the concrete meaning of these norms in specific circumstances.

Implicit in the meaning of democracy are the values of dignity, self-determination, intelligence, pluralism, and cohesion (or community). Democracy is itself a value network in which all paths lead to the ground of dignity. To teach in a democratic setting is to deal with the implications of democratic values on a daily basis. The nature of values and moral education is intimately linked to the nature of democracy. Teachers need a firm understanding of the value dimensions of democratic society if they are to be effective moral educators.

Moral Education in a Democratic Society

Democratic values serve as ends in education, as well as casting light on its means. A teacher who believes in the rights of self-determination and rationality cannot see the school's role in terms of the imposition or indoctrination of values. The teacher must appeal to the students' reason and not rest content with merely conditioning student behavior. In this view, the fundamental purpose of education is the development of intelligence. Teachers have a responsibility to transmit the moral values of democracy, but they must do so in a way that makes the values reasonable to believe for the student. As Israel Scheffler has written:

> To teach, in the standard sense, is at some points, at least, to submit oneself to the understanding and independent judgment of the pupil, to his demand for reasons, to his sense of what constitutes an adequate explanation. To teach someone that such-and-such is the case is not merely to try to get him to believe it. . . . Teaching involves further that . . . we try also to get him to believe it for reasons that within the limits of his capacity to grasp, are our reasons. Teaching, in this way, requires us to reveal our reasons to the student, and, by so doing, to submit them to his evaluation and criticism. . . .[6]

THE SCHOOL AND AESTHETIC VALUES

Shaver maintains that aesthetic standards are private and subjective. From his vantage point, there is no ultimate or objective beauty; nor is there any compelling reason why society should endorse a single set of standards for judging beauty. While teachers should expose students to art that is sophisticated in form and universal in significance, they must be careful not to absolutize what are, after all, merely contingent artistic preferences. Shaver implies that aesthetic values express what is beautiful in one's own eyes, not what is right between people. Aesthetic values must not be regarded as obligatory; they are matters of individual taste. Students need to study a variety of aesthetic forms, styles, and criteria in order to have an adequate base from which to construct their own aesthetic values. But traditional conceptions of beauty should never be confused with moral imperatives.

INSTRUMENTAL VALUES

As with aesthetic values, teachers need to guard against subtle transitions from instrumental to moral judgments. That is, they must take care that means do not become ends in themselves. The rules and procedures of the school and classroom should be functionally related to the learning teachers and students seek. Maintaining a set seating pattern, a "pass" system to go to the lavatory, punishments for tardiness, or demerits for talking out of turn are justified only when they promote learning and are consistent with a commitment to dignity.

Self-examination about means-ends relationships may encourage teachers to relax unnecessary behavioral controls. Scrutinizing instrumental values, moreover, is a first step toward discussing these values with students. To clarify and justify instrumental standards is to suggest they would pass muster in a public inspection, that most people would find them acceptable if they were to consider them carefully. Armed with a clear rationale, open inquiry with students regarding the functions of instrumental values may seem less threatening to the teacher and more constructive. Teachers who are clear about their own values and the relationships among them find it easier to share those values with students. Having a firm rationale for instrumental values does not, of course, mean that students will never challenge those values. "But it does mean that such challenges can lead to rational means-ends discussions, rather than to shouted invectives, or the quiet but seething confrontations so common in schools." [7]

MORAL VALUES

Moral values are primary, in Shaver's view; they are of higher priority in values education than are aesthetic or instrumental values. As aesthetic choices begin to impinge on others, moral questions are suggested. For example, a teacher may require students, in spite of their resistance, to examine works of art she finds worthy. Is the teacher morally justified in requiring the students to study the art? Instrumental values, for their part, are ultimately accountable to the moral values they are designed to serve. The first-order status of moral principles applies to teaching in every field, not merely in areas where an emphasis on citizen education makes moral values particularly relevant.

RATIONALE BUILDING IN PRACTICE

Shaver is careful not to propose a specific program for moral education, but he does suggest some basic considerations directly relevant to moral instruction. These considerations include the processes of value identification and values clarification, label generalization, value conflict analysis, and qualified decision making.

The Identification and Clarification of Values

Values help shape our behavior. They give consistency and congruence to our lives. But they also create dissonance and contradiction. As we noted, our clusters of values—economic, aesthetic, moral, and instrumental—may stand in tension with one another. We may value discipline and competence at work and spontaneity and playfulness at home. We may affirm the ideal of human equality but expect our children to marry within their religion and race. We may stand for equality before the law but cherish special attention from our friends. Exploring the connections among our values is an important step in the direction of self-awareness and self-mastery. We need to ask ourselves what are values are, how strongly we feel about them, and how they function as a whole. This self-searching applies with equal force to students. Locating and surfacing value commitments is a process Shaver calls "value identification." In essence, value identification is a parallel process to values clarification, which is discussed in chapter 5.

Because values are dimensional categories that are often at odds with one another, in Shaver's framework they cannot be fully identified and clarified unless they are examined in concrete situations of choice. For example, a student may single out the ideal of "equal protection of the laws" as a core value. What does this value mean? Does it mean that students should be bused to achieve racial integration? Does it apply when homosexuals seek fair treatment in housing and employment practices? One's interpretation of "equal protection of the laws" is neither simple nor static. It is crucial that teachers help their students go beyond a superficial identification of values.

Label Generalization

Shaver maintains that in a democratic society, moral education should teach students to see their values in the context of basic democratic, moral norms. The process of placing specific value issues in a general legal-moral framework is termed *label generalization*.

Here, Shaver is suggesting that students ought to be helped to view value conflicts in terms of the principles laid down in the U.S. Constitution. He is much less concerned with personal value conflicts (e.g., between love and work, dependence and independence, or self-realization and family responsibility) than with public controversies, or with value conflicts that arise within the classroom. Students need to be taught to relate their unsophisticated value concepts to the underlying precepts of democratic government.

Shaver is well aware that the informal vocabulary people use in applying their values to concrete situations often seems entirely different from the formal language of moral and legal discourse. Yet he suggests that this difference is commonly more apparent than real. For example, consider the idea of fairness, which children develop in play and in class. "It's not fair" may be said of a playground game in which, by some covert conspiracy, the finest student athletes arrange to be on the same team. Or "It's not fair" may be invoked to protest a referee who discriminates against a team. Shaver observes that here the idea of fairness resembles the political-legal concept of equal treatment before the law. Similarly, a child who retorts, "I've got a right to say what I want," when an adult silences him is invoking a value that might be termed freedom of speech. The moral values of democracy provide a framework within which many, if not most, interpersonal value issues can be analyzed.

Label generalization is crucial because it helps students become fluent in the moral language of the democratic community. It opens them to a common channel of debate and decision making. In Shaver's words:

Helping students to begin to use labels with basic value meanings serves several related instructional and societal functions: (1) It provides a basis for value identification and clarification. (2) It gives students a more powerful conceptual scheme as they relate their own untutored commitments to the basic values of the society. (3) It gives students a more powerful value language for analysis, discussion, and persuasion. And (4) it helps to insure a nationwide values vocabulary at the basic value level among people who, unlike news commentators, politicians, and lawyers, frequently would not otherwise use such terms in their thinking and disputes. In short, the process of label generalization is important because it relates the student's own developing value vocabulary and conceptual schema to the broader and more powerful basic values of a democratic society.[8]

As an example of a classroom discussion in which the process of label generalization would be meaningful, consider the following hypothetical transcript from a lesson on current events:

Problem. *Focus on the value of "fairness" as you read this section.*

A news item I read to my ninth-grade homeroom said that a white college student had been denied admission to law school because the institution had a "quota" system—a system that gave preferential admissions to minority students. The white student was suing the school because his qualifying entrance scores were higher than those of blacks who had gained admission.

"What's your reaction?" I asked.

Dick Simmons was grinning from ear to ear. "That white dude, he knows what it's like now! About time, too!"

"What do you mean?"

"Oh, you know, man! Step to the back of the bus and all that jive? So let the honky sweat it out—be good for him! Like maybe it'll build his *character*, you know?" Dick's voice was drawling and sarcastic.

I glanced around the room. Joanie Anderson's face was pink with anger. Her hand stabbed into the tense quiet Dick had created.

"Well, I don't think it's *fair*," she blurted out. "I mean . . ."

"*Fair!*" Dick interrupted in a half-shout. He swung round in his desk. "You gonna talk about *fair* to me? Huh? You think

Whitey was talking *fairness* and all that honky crap when they sent the slave ships over? You think working blacks on the plantations was *fair*? Or breaking up the families? Or white masters screwing the black women? You think being denied the right to vote was *fair*? Or segregated housing and restaurants and schools?" Dick let the questions hang and then drove in his point. "Hey, baby—you *owe* us—and you better get used to payin' up!"

Joe Sheridan didn't even bother to raise his hand. "Dick, you're full of it. Joanie don't own you *nothing*. And neither do I. Nobody owes nobody—that's what I think."

Dick's sneer was cool and stylized. "Four hundred years, dig? That's what you owing blacks in this country!" His fist went up in the clenched symbol of black power. "Ain't no way you gonna turn back the clock!"

The challenge was unmistakable in Dick's voice. "That's true," I said. "Whites can't turn back the clock and neither can blacks. That's the terrible thing about our history. But it's also the great thing, too, because it shows us how far we've really come in the past few years."

"Blacks ain't been nowhere 'cept down the river," Dick said.

"I don't know," I shrugged. "I mean, look at this news clipping we've been discussing. Why, ten or fifteen years ago we couldn't have had this kind of talk."

Dick's eyes snapped with anger. "And you know why? 'Cause niggers hadn't learned how to play with matches yet!"

"You could have a point," I conceded. "Maybe that's what convinced *some* white politicians. But what about everyday people like Joanie and Joe? What about me? Do you think that burning down our places would encourage us to support the black movement?"

Dick fell silent as he chewed over my question for a moment. "Let's talk over this value of fairness," I added. "Maybe this kind of discussion can help us work things out for ourselves in the future."

Follow-up. *Dick and the other students who entered into the discussion seem to have different meanings for the value*

*of "fairness." Can you identify the various definitions—such
as justice, equality of opportunity, retribution—and whom
they fit? Which are basic democratic values?*

*How would you work with this class to help them identify
and clarify their commitments and relate them to basic value
labels?* [9]

Value Conflict Analysis

Moral judgments necessarily involve value conflict. Examine
the consequences of acting on a moral value and you will invariably discover that another moral ideal is compromised. When
students weigh the implications, the possible consequences, of
their moral decisions, they need to view moral concepts as dimensional rather than categorical constructs. That is, they must
learn to treat moral values as degrees of desirable conditions
along a continuum, rather than as all-or-nothing command-
ments. For example, you may value freedom of speech yet place
limits on its expression. Who would uphold the right to shout
"Fire!" in a crowded theater as a prank? Similarly, you may
affirm the standard of majority rule but recognize the need for
protection of minority rights. Or you may believe in the free
market but support government-backed antipollution measures
or homeowner loans. Value commitments are seldom pure and
absolute. But one value may yield some ground to another and
still preserve its basic meaning.

Shaver contends that value dilemmas often need to be en-
gineered by the teacher in the classroom. Particularly in a
homogeneous classroom, the conditions of pluralism must be
deliberately created. "To bring out different points of view, you
may have to take a devil's advocate position, or use student role
play, films, or outside readings." [10] Students cannot learn to
deal with value conflicts unless conflict is present or can be
evoked.

Although in the rationale building model Shaver does not
work out a complete procedure for analyzing value conflicts, a
strategy he suggested in another context relates centrally to
conflict analysis: the use of analogous cases. In *Teaching Public*

Issues in the High School, which Shaver co-authored with Donald Oliver, the role of the analogous case is made clear:

> The purpose of constructing analogies is to force an antagonist to compare a number of similar situations to which he reacts inconsistently. If the comparison is to be useful, the situations must embrace conflicting values both of which are likely to be favored. For example, while most of us support the actions of the English colonists in America during the American Revolution, probably few of us would support a comparable action by the Negroes in Mississippi, although the issue is similar. . . . The person is then forced to change one position or to rationalize the apparent inconsistency by seeking criteria which differentiate the two seemingly similar cases.[11]

The challenge of analogous cases is fundamental for bringing into focus the principles at stake in a value conflict. Students should be able to see value issues in terms of basic democratic norms and apply these norms consistently in complex situations.

Qualified Decision Making

The search for criteria, or principles, by which to distinguish two situations characterized by the same conflicting values should lead to a qualified decision stating under what circumstances priority will be given to one value or the other. The need to make qualified, rather than categorical, value judgments grows out of the need to treat values as dimensional concepts. A qualified decision is "one that takes into account the possible negative consequences of a policy or action to be supported, and the circumstances under which you might change your mind and support a different value."[12] The process of working toward a general qualified position is illustrated by the following example:

Americans of Japanese ancestry on the west coast were forcibly relocated shortly after the attack on Pearl Harbor in 1941. Let us assume that we support the relocation, seeing in the situation a value conflict between certain freedoms guaranteed to all citizens, in this case the right to due process under law, as against the security of the community or nation. We then think of an analogy which reverses our position. Suppose there are five Americans of Japanese ancestry in a community. One is seen commiting a murder. The witnesses who observe the crime from a distance know only that the murderer had Oriental physical characteristics. Should all five men who have Oriental physical characteristics be locked up to protect the security of the community? Most of us would answer "no." It is the same dilemma, however; the security of the community versus denial of due process. How do we explain our inconsistency? We might say that "security" of the nation or community has two different meanings. In the Japanese relocation case, the legal framework of government which guarantees our basic rights was threatened; in the murder case, while perhaps some citizens' lives were jeopardized by allowing all suspects to go free for lack of evidence, the government itself was not threatened. We then arrive at a general position: The government can justifiably deny citizens basic rights only when that government itself, which is committed to protect those rights, is threatened with destruction; otherwise the action is wrong. This is not to say that one cannot argue convincingly the opposite position, and qualify it in another way.[13]

What Shaver means by a "qualified general position" is essentially equivalent to what value analysis calls "stating the principle implicit in the value decision" (see chapter 6). Both formulations stress that in practical terms, even the ideal of dignity is expressed as a blend or balance of values achieved through compromise. For example, a respect for individual dignity is reflected in the values of liberty and equality. Nevertheless, in specific situations the overall standard of dignity may represent a tradeoff between these two values. To reach a qualified position, to use the terms of the rationale building model, is to zero-in on the particular conditions that make one value more relevant than another, and to state these conditions in the form of a general proposition or policy statement. In other words, students do not merely deduce a conclusion from a single value; they must show how the conclusion represents a tradeoff between competing values. Thus, instead of reaching a global judgment like "Political revolutions are wrong," a student might conclude as follows: "Whenever a major governmental force is working successfully to reduce inequalities among citizens, and whenever there is a realistic chance that they will eventually be removed, it is better to stay within the legal framework of government." [14] Or, instead of stopping at the generalization "I believe in free speech," the student might decide, "Free speech should be guaranteed under all circumstances except when such freedom presents a clear and present danger of inducing violence to others."

It is no coincidence that Shaver's earlier work in values education was called the "jurisprudential" approach. For the process of reaching a qualified decision, on the basis of the values of democracy, is akin to the process a judge goes through in reaching a verdict on a case. Shaver also emphasizes that just as legal precedents often need revision in the light of new situations, so, too, must students realize that their positions are conditional in nature. The ultimate principle of human dignity is not subject to change, but the specific embodiments of that principle are. Students, like judges, need to keep an open mind.

Affective or Nonverbal Aspects of Moral Education

Values education in a democratic society involves helping students develop an analytic frame for the assessment and resolution of value conflicts. But teachers are also obliged to foster the emotional commitment of students to the democratic creed. Since emotional commitments tend to be formed at an early age, as Shaver observes, it is especially important that in the elementary grades learning activities be designed to exemplify in a dramatic or experiential way the essential place of moral values (e.g., by a dramatization of the John Peter Zenger free press episode). Young children may not be able to build an abstract rationale for value judgments. But Shaver points out that students do not learn moral values solely through reasoned debate. They may learn by example and from behavioral reinforcement. For example, if a teacher praises students for helping one another understand their assignments, the children may come to value cooperative learning. Or students who consistently see the teacher listening respectfully to everybody's point of view may adopt this practice too. Teachers need to show young children how to be fair in concrete ways, for children seem to learn situation-specific rules of behavior before they are able to grasp universal principles of justice. Such rules as waiting one's turn in line, raising one's hand before talking, sharing clean-up duties, or refraining from name calling may be considered important for the children's own welfare even if the abstract justification for such rules is not completely understood. Ultimately, Shaver emphasizes, the goal of moral education is the development of independent moral thinking. But, even in the moral domain, youngsters learn to walk before they can run. For instance, they learn not to hit their peers when they disagree with them before they learn the concept of tolerance. Shaver is thus not insensitive to the auxiliary role that habit training may play in the education of the very young.

SUMMARY AND APPRAISAL

Shaver's approach to moral education emphasizes the teacher's need to understand the nature of democratic society, the teacher's role in such a society, and the nature of values. He is concerned with helping teachers build rationales for making educational decisions in general and for teaching the concepts and skills of democratic citizenship in particular. Although he constructs a logic of procedure for moral education, he offers no pedagogical blueprint. The teacher is to help the student develop a democratic frame for the identification, clarification, and analysis of values and value conflicts. In the long run, the students' approach to values issues should be as explicit and coherent as the teacher's.

The strength of Shaver's model is its linkage of the theory of democracy to the practice of moral education. No other approach analyzes democratic values and their implications for teaching in such depth. The rationale building framework helps us see why moral education is so important and suggests the overall direction such education must take in a democratic setting.

In spite of the overall soundness of Shaver's work, several elements in the model invite refinement. His use of the "instrumental value" concept seems unnecessarily confusing, and his definition of the "personal preference" level of moral values is unclear and misleading. More fundamentally, although he makes overtures toward an integration of cognitive developmental theory with his model, Shaver does not spell out how his approach could be adapted to elementary school children, except to suggest that teachers rely on indirect, nonverbal techniques of modeling and behavioral reinforcement to supplement rational discussion. Shaver asserts that he is not primarily concerned with explicating a pedagogy, but such a concern might be in order, at least in discussing instruction for young children.

Shaver acknowledges that his definition of instrumental value is unorthodox. Traditionally, an instrumental value is distinguished from an end or a fundamental value, not from aesthetic and moral values. The class of instrumental value, in the conventional view, does not exclude the class of aesthetic or moral value; instrumental values may be aesthetic or moral standards. Symmetry, balance, and harmony, for example, may be seen as both aesthetic and instrumental values, for they express aesthetic principles and also serve the larger end of beauty. What defines an instrumental value, according to general usage, is its function in relation to other values, not the particular domain of experience (such as aesthetics or morality) to which it is applied. An instrumental value is commonly considered a means, not a specific kind of means.

Shaver chooses to regard instrumental values as a separate category on the grounds that the distinction brings into sharper focus differences between values issues in education and the tendency to moralize about aesthetic and instrumental values.[15] But Shaver's concept may confuse more than it clarifies. He, himself, argues that all values in the democratic ethos are at once moral and instrumental.[16] Moral values toward the "personal preference" end of the moral values continuum obviously serve an instrumental capacity with regard to middle-level and basic values. The reader must thus juggle the categories of instrumental, moral, moral-instrumental, personal preference, middle-level, and basic moral value. Why not consider all values pertaining to good character or right action to be moral values? Instrumental moral values could then include such values as honesty, courage, charity, and cooperativeness, which are derived from the fundamental values of justice and benevolence. This would not alter the substance of Shaver's position, but it might make his terminology more manageable.

Shaver's treatment of moral values might also be improved by clarifying the relationship between "personal preference" values and "matters of personal taste." On the one hand, Shaver argues that moral values can never be reduced to considerations of taste alone: "Because moral values are used to justify and judge ethical decisions, and these have impact on other people, moral standards are not merely matters of personal taste." [17] On the other hand, Shaver defines one class of moral values ("the least significant") as "personal preferences." Expressions of such values may well be preceded by such phrases as "I just prefer. . . ." Shaver never makes clear what precisely is the difference between personal taste and personal preference. Both appear to reflect psychological, rather than objective, qualities. That is, each says more about the sensibilities of the individual than about the practice or action under consideration. On what grounds can solitude and cleanliness be considered moral values? Shaver suggests that they serve as moral values when we use them to justify our behavior toward other people. But in that case, solitude and cleanliness become interpersonal and not merely subjective standards. To say that a person *should* be clean is to imply that cleanliness is in itself a good and not merely a matter of individual like or dislike. Shaver seems to confuse the grounds of moral values on the "personal preference" level with the concept of personal taste, in spite of his claim to the contrary.

In addition to these elements of internal inconsistency, Shaver's model might be questioned from the perspective of cognitive developmentalism. Shaver acknowledges the warnings of developmentalists about the limits of children's facility for abstraction at given ages. And, as noted, he devotes considerable attention to nonverbal forms of moral education such as teaching by example and behavioral management. Yet Shaver is critical of Kohlberg, apparently for underestimating the cognitive range of elementary school children. Shaver states: "Some people have argued that if it is frustrating—as Kohlberg suggests—for students to be confronted by moral reasoning more than one stage above their own level, then teaching decisions based on a stage 5 rationale may be inappropriate, even counterproductive. We would argue that, on the contrary, one reason many people do not reach stages 5 and 6 is that the school does not provide an environment that encourages moral development." [18]

Shaver's argument confuses several issues. First, it is not clear what he means by "teaching decisions based on a stage 5 rationale." Presumably, teachers, as mature and reflective adults, will seek to ground their moral decisions in stage 5 principles. Kohlberg would hardly disagree with this. Indeed, cognitive developmentalism would hold that it is only when teachers understand children's needs in a systematic and comprehensive way that they can do justice to them. Second, Kohlberg is in wholehearted agreement with Shaver's claim that the school does not provide an environment that encourages moral development to stages 5 and 6. Much of Kohlberg's work in recent years has tried to show that improving the justice structure of the school can have substantial impact on students' moral reasoning (see chapter 7).

What is Shaver's bone of contention? Implicit in his critique of Kohlberg is the suggestion that young students could learn to operate at stage 5—perhaps think in the abstract terms of the U.S. Constitution—if only they were taught to do so. Shaver seems to imply that the process of abstracting values from concrete situations, reasoning analogously, formulating consistent criteria, and developing a qualified general position—a process that demands stage 5 thinking—could be part of the curriculum for elementary and junior high students if we made a sincere commitment to the goals of moral education. This may be true, but Shaver does little to show in a specific way how preadolescents could be taught abstract reasoning. He offers no evidence to support his claim, and compelling data cast doubts on its validity. How Shaver's pedagogy can be adapted to children remains unclear.

We have pointed to a few areas where Shaver's theory may lack clarity or support. Nevertheless, the rationale building model provides a secure framework for a program in moral education. Shaver presents a coherent and incisive account of the nature of values, the principles of democracy, and the analytic demands of democratic citizenship. Because the model establishes such a broad context for moral education, it well serves as a point of departure for the approaches that follow.

REFERENCES

Principal Source

Shaver, James, and William Strong. *Facing Value Decisions: Rationale Building for Teachers.* Belmont, Calif.: Wadsworth, 1976.

This book describes the rationale building approach and is designed to facilitate teacher reflection on the role of a values educator. Specific exercises are included to assist the teacher in this process.

Related Readings

Newmann, F. M., and D. W. Oliver. *Clarifying Public Controversy: An Approach to Teaching Social Studies.* Boston: Little, Brown, 1970.

Oliver, D. W., and J. P. Shaver. *Teaching Public Issues in the High School.* Logan, Utah: Utah State University, 1974.

Shaver, J. P. *Instructor's Manual: The Analysis of Public Issues Program.* Boston: Houghton Mifflin, 1973.

Shaver, James P., and A. Guy Larkins. *Decision Making in a Democracy.* Boston: Houghton Mifflin, 1973.

Shaver, James P., and A. Guy Larkins. *The Analysis of Public Issues Program.* Boston: Houghton Mifflin, 1973.

The public issues program originally developed by Oliver, Shaver, and Newmann focuses on developing student skills in analyzing and discussing critical social issues. After their initial work on the project, the program's authors developed somewhat different interests. Oliver and Newmann, in particular, shifted to other concerns: Oliver became more interested with the meaning and development of community, and Newmann focused on the citizen action program described in chapter 8 of this book.

4
THE CONSIDERATION MODEL

The rationale building model emphasized the importance of reason and judgment in moral education. Although Shaver discussed the role of affective attachments in moral development, affect clearly took a back seat to cognition in his approach. In this chapter we deal with an approach to moral education in which moral sentiments are front and center. Based on the Schools Moral Education Curriculum Project in Britain, Peter McPhail and his associates have authored the Lifeline series, which is published in both British and North American versions. The teachers guide to Lifeline is entitled *Learning to Care*.[1] And it is with caring, rather than with judging, that McPhail is primarily concerned.

The aims of the Lifeline series are so wide-ranging that they are difficult to pin down. Moral education in McPhail's program deals with morality on the broadest basis, as part of the total personality and social structure. In McPhail's view, moral education should not be reduced to an analysis of rules and prohibitions. Rather, it should focus on a person's general style of relating to self and others. More specifically, Lifeline seeks to demonstrate that "in practice, living for others is rewarding, is motivating, and can be described in a real sense as living for oneself." Ultimately, in McPhail's scheme, moral education aims to free individuals from "those destructive and self-destructive impulses that may masquerade as individuality—to egocentricity and narcissism, to selfishness and surliness and those other traits that develop in response to the unhappy and unhealthy society and hamper the true personality from expressing its creative and productive needs."

For McPhail, moral education must work toward the liberation of the individual from the shackles of fear and distrust. To empower the student to give and receive love, at least in the sense of brotherly love, is McPhail's guiding purpose. In the consideration model, moral education is seen as embracing the total personality.

THEORY

The Lifeline program is based in large part on an intensive study of adolescent students' needs, conducted from 1967 to 1971. More than eight hundred English secondary school students between the ages of thirteen and eighteen were asked "critical incident" questions. Either through personally administered questionnaires or in interviews, they were asked to cite one example of a situation in which an adult had treated them well and one example in which an adult had treated them badly. In further surveys supplemental questions were asked regarding peer relations. The investigation revealed a common view among teen-agers of "good" incidents. Positive incidents reflected the qualities of consideration, humor, and the willingness to compromise. A shared relationship was good; domination was bad, although a few passive personalities welcomed others who would make decisions for them. The message from the research seemed clear and unequivocal to McPhail: "good treatment shows consideration for one's needs, feelings, and interests; bad treatment indicates the reverse."

McPhail's study expressed his conviction that "if you want to know what people need and how to meet that need, the first step is to ask them to identify and articulate their problems as they see them and not to tell them what their problems are. The boys' and girls' own use of good and bad in the surveys showed us how the ought of morality should come from the is of reality."

Because he found so much evidence in the students' responses of a commitment to openness, reciprocity, and caring in interpersonal relations, McPhail interpreted the research as proof "that the fundamental human need is to get along with others, to love and be loved, and that it is a prime responsibility of organized education to help meet this need." On the whole, students felt that school placed too much stress on accumulating and manipulating information and gave too little attention to helping them resolve questions about personal identity and social relations. McPhail, then, places great stock in the perceptions and attitudes of students themselves in defining the purpose of moral education. Indeed, he implies that the most compelling reason for initiating a moral education program is that students feel the need for one.

McPhail takes care to point out that most adolescents are able to distinguish between freedom and license. At least in the surveys, students suggested that while they certainly wanted freedom in making choices and reaching decisions, they welcomed the aid of sensitive adults. Moreover, the teen-agers indicated an admiration for adults who provided a "good example" and lived up to the standards they professed, even when those standards were disagreeable to the young people. Parents and teachers who showed conviction and integrity were preferred to those who tried to maintain neutrality by "fence sitting." Based on the questionnaire and interview data, McPhail concluded that adolescents seem "capable of making fine distinction between firmness and stubbornness, between a position born of conviction and one based on dogma. Impartiality is appreciated, for instance, in an adult chairing a discussion, but in most situations, identifying attitudes and beliefs is considered helpful to the development of individuality." Students are open to learning from adults; what they resent is being dominated by them.

While McPhail reveals a great deal of respect for adolescent social attitudes, he is not blind to the immaturity that characterizes many teen-agers' responses to social problems. This immaturity is particularly noticeable in the responses of young teen-agers. In fact, McPhail conducted an additional study, with a sample of two hundred boys and girls aged twelve to eighteen, to look for a relationship between age and maturity of social judgment. "Maturity" in this study was assessed in terms of the typical responses given by fifty adults in a predominantly middle-class sample in which the adults were asked the same questions posed to teen-agers. To define maturity in this way is, of course, to endorse the values of the dominant culture. McPhail is aware that equating middle-class norms with maturity of judgment is a somewhat arbitrary connection, but he feels it is appropriate in this context.

In any event, thirteen social situations involving adolescents and their peers, parents, and other adults were presented to the subjects in a questionnaire. McPhail grouped the responses in several categories ranging from "passive" through "aggressive" to "mature imaginative." Although he fails to elaborate on the definition of each category, he does provide sample responses that fit the categories. For example,

Situation. *A boy or girl of your own age, with whom you are friendly, appears to be very upset for some reason unknown to you. You would:*

1.	Do nothing	Passive
2.	Feel disturbed but not know what to do	Passive emotional
3.	Point out the situation to some adult	Adult-dependent
4.	Talk to your friends about it.	Peer-dependent
5.	Tell the person concerned to pull himself/ herself together.	Aggressive
6.	Make fun of that boy or girl	Very aggressive
7.	Avoid him/her.	Avoidance
8.	Try asking your friend what is the matter.	Experimental crude

9. Attempt to talk to him/her as if you have not noticed that anything is wrong.   Experimental sophisticated

10. Comfort your friend.   Mature conventional

11. Set about interesting the person concerned in something that is going on, at the same time being available to help if asked.   Mature imaginative

McPhail reports data for experimental and mature responses only. As one might expect, for both boys and girls the frequency of mature responses increased steadily from age twelve to age eighteen. Experimental responses peaked for girls at fourteen and for boys at fifteen. By eighteen years of age mature responses were about twice as common as experimental ones for both sexes.

From this research McPhail concluded that "it is a valid and useful way of describing adolescence to designate it as an age of social experiment between puberty and the time when the individual is ready to cope with adult problems and assume adult responsibilities." Curiously, McPhail neglected to explain exactly why he inferred from the frequency of "experimental" responses to hypothetical situations that adolescence was a period of social experiment. This is odd for two reasons. First, as McPhail acknowledges, students' stated preferences for verbal responses in hypothetical cases is hardly a definitive test of the quality of their social judgment. Students tend to be more altruistic on questionnaires than in real life. Second, since McPhail chooses not to define in any extended way his concept of "experimental" response, it is difficult to see a connection between such a response and the general characteristic or style of experimental thinking and acting.

These objections notwithstanding, McPhail suggests that one aim of the Lifeline series is to promote the development of mature social judgment and behavior. And his concept of maturity seems to refer to an individual's disposition and ability to help a needy person generate meaningful solutions to a social predicament. In short, maturity is seen as creative caring.

Teaching Students to Care

McPhail introduces the teachers guide to the Lifeline series with a quotation from John Ruskin: "Education does not mean teaching people to know what they do not know; it means teaching them to behave as they do not behave." This statement reflects a central theme in McPhail's work: moral education is as concerned with cultivating dispositions and shaping behavior as it is with developing problem-solving abilities. According to McPhail, we learn moral values by observing how significant people in our lives treat us and others. Indeed, morality is "contagious," something we pick up by being around considerate people. "A pupil learns more from what a teacher is and does," McPhail insists, "than from what a teacher teaches. . . ." Learning from the example of others is the "keystone in the natural development of individuals." The importance of observational learning and social modeling cannot be overemphasized, McPhail maintains. Higher-level moral thinking, as well as moral behavior, needs to be modeled for students in lifelike situations.

> Behavior and attitudes are "contagious," in a psychological sense, and there is much truth in the maxim that morals are caught, and not taught. But *example* is a form of education, perhaps its highest form. (As the English historian Lord Acton once observed, Plato in all his learned dialogues was unable to define the nature of justice satisfactorily, so he wrote the dialogues around the noble character of Socrates, recognizing that in his person and his life, Socrates *demonstrated* what a just man should be, even though the abstraction eludes precise definition.) If we appreciate the nature of social conditioning, reason is increased and rationalization decreases.

McPhail describes in substantial detail the characteristics of the morally "contagious" classroom and the morally exemplary teacher. His ideal classroom is a therapeutic one in which "suspicion, wariness, defensiveness, hostility and anxiety" gradually disappear. To illustrate the quality of teacher-student interaction, which nurtures moral growth, he cites the following passage from Maslow's classic study *Motivation and Personality:*

> [The teacher-subjects] behaved in a very unneurotic way simply by interpreting the whole situation differently, e.g., as a pleasant collaboration rather than as a clash of wills; the replacement of artificial dignity—that is easily and inevitably threatened—with the natural simplicity that is *not* easily threatened; the giving up of the attempt to be omniscient and omnipotent; the absence of student-threatening, authoritarianism; the refusal to regard the students as competing with each other or with the teacher; the refusal to assume the professor stereotype and the insistence of remaining as realistically human as, say, a plumber or a carpenter.[2]

McPhail clearly considers himself a humanistic educator, in the spirit of Maslow and Carl Rogers. In the voice of humanism, McPhail speaks of the need for personal authenticity, insight, and creativity. At the same time, he seems to accept wholeheartedly the theory and practice of social conditioning, which focuses on training socially acceptable behavior rather than developing independent and imaginative thinking. McPhail writes that "every human being is conditioned from the moment he or she draws the first breath as a baby. . . . Young people are conditioned in behavior every day, by every teacher, policeman, shopkeeper, coach, friend, or enemy they have contact with. But nearly all conditioning is done in ignorance." The implication is that teachers are to condition students from a position of knowledge. Yet, as we shall see later in this chapter, it is not clear how the techniques of conditioning (reinforcing appropriate behavior in a systematic manner) in and of themselves can serve the cause of personal integration and autonomy. McPhail speaks of behaviorism and humanism in the same breath, without taking time to clarify the relationship between the two.

What McPhail is clear about is his opposition to highly rationalized approaches to moral education, which require students to wrestle with tough questions of moral obligation. "One especially destructive feature of some German rationalist and Western Protestant thinking has been the notion that morality must in some way hurt—the more bitter the medicine, the more beneficial the dose—or that no decision qualifies as moral unless the individual really does not want to make it or carry it out. Such attitudes perhaps gave rise to the familiar half-comic, half-complaining remark, Everything I like is either illegal, immoral, or fattening!"

To McPhail, morality involves more a personality style than a mode of reasoning. He uses the term "moral style," which he defines as a way of behaving that is "genuinely affiliative," to represent the essence of moral functioning. Morality here is less a matter of balancing conflicting claims than it is the fulfillment of an individual's natural harmony with others. Education in the "considerate style of life" does not rely on "persuading students to accept rationally that it is right to treat others with consideration. . . . Effective education itself is learning to care because it demonstrates the considerate style of life in action and thus motivates students to adopt it because it is experienced as a rewarding and attractive way of living and relating to others." Moral education in the consideration model aims to show the student that the caring way is the pleasant way. No other model makes such a claim, at least in so direct a form.

PRACTICE

Although McPhail affirms in the theory section of *Learning to Care* that "relationships are more important than materials" in moral education, the Lifeline program does include an extensive series of instructional products, which have been field-tested in British classrooms with more than twenty thousand students. Although the curriculum is intended for secondary schools, the reading level of even the most advanced material is within the reach of many fifth and sixth graders.

Lifeline is divided into three sections, which present students with progressively more complex social situations. These situations generally place heavier intellectual demands on the student than one might expect in view of McPhail's disdain for self-consciously rational forms of moral education. In fact, when we compare McPhail's specific objectives for Lifeline with his global pronouncements on moral development, we see that the objectives are compatible with the more intellectually oriented models treated in this book (e.g., those of Shaver, Kohlberg, and Coombs). Lifeline is designed to encourage observation and understanding of all the cues, verbal and nonverbal, that are pointers to people's needs, interests, and feelings. The program also seeks to sharpen students' ability to calculate and predict the consequences of actions, as well as to foster the acquisition of scientific knowledge relevant to the understanding of consequences. Finally, Lifeline is meant to have a "holistic impact; that is, it is much concerned with bringing together facts, ideals, skills, and experiences that bear on decisions affecting men and women. It is vitally important in decision making to be able to cross the boundaries between subject disciplines and to relate and combine the fullest knowledge." Reason and knowledge thus play essential roles in the consideration model, even if they are downplayed in certain aspects of the theory.

Each section of Lifeline encompasses a number of individual units. Section 1, *In Other People's Shoes*, has three units: *Sensitivity*, *Consequences*, and *Points of View*. The situations in this section are built around common interpersonal problems experienced in the home, school, or neighborhood. The second section, *Proving the Rule*, has five component units: *Rules and Individuals*, *What Do You Expect?*, *Who Do You Think I Am?*, *In Whose Interests?*, and *Why Should I?* These units move from comparatively simple instances of pressures and conflicts in personal relations to more complex conflicts of group interests and the problem of authority. In section 3, *What Would You Have Done?*, students encounter dramatic moral predicaments based on actual events in history. The six booklets in this section are *Birth Day*, *Solitary Confinement*, *Arrest!*, *Street Scene*, *Tragedy*, and *Gale in the Hospital*. The purpose of these materials is to widen the students' moral perspective beyond the immediate society and encourage the development of a deeper, more universal frame of judgment.

In Other People's Shoes

The aim of this section of Lifeline is "to begin where the motivation is and to concentrate on developing the consideration for others that exists in everyone, in however small measure, so that it extends to a growing circle." McPhail writes that the materials and strategies in this first section share these features:

1. The material is situational.
2. The situations are derived from survey work with adolescents. These are *their* situations.
3. The statement of the situations is brief to encourage individuals to make them their own by supplying personal details if they have been in such situations themselves.
4. The questions asked generally concern doing rather than theorizing.
5. Role play and dramatic representation of suggested courses of action is generally preferred to discussion as being more likely to promote emotional as well as rational involvement and therefore as furthering more realistic appreciation and understanding of human behavior.
6. The adolescent's natural inclination to experiment socially is encouraged.
7. The basic motivation for considerate behavior provided for in the use of the material is the disposition to consider others, which results in rewarding feedback.
8. The lists of incidents are open-ended and indicative of what teachers and students can do on their own.
9. The situations should not be worked through or used continuously until they are exhausted. Student choices should be introduced whenever possible because involvement is essential.
10. The situations in *In Other People's Shoes* should never be used for punishment or extra work.

UNIT 1: *SENSITIVITY*

This unit consists of forty-six person-to-person situations cited by adolescents in the survey research as being both important and problematic. Each situation is depicted by a lively color drawing that appears on a "sensitivity card." Below the drawing is the question "What do you do?" This basic question is asked after every situation so that a student can state, role-play, mime, describe in writing, paint, or discuss in a group what he or she would do in the case at hand. McPhail stresses that the teacher should not rely exclusively on verbal responses because "valid personal and social learning depend on emotional as well as verbal response."

Below are several examples of situations found in the sensitivity cards:

You know that your best friend is doing something which is causing him or her to suffer. What do you do?

Your mother, who is tired and distracted by a younger child, is not listening to something important you are trying to tell her. What do you do?

You lend a coat to your cousin; when the coat is returned, there is a cigarette burn in the lapel. What do you do?

An acquaintance of yours often butts in and tries to change the subject when you are talking to someone. What do you do? [3]

For each situation, McPhail has outlined typical student responses, which he categorizes in terms of the moral taxonomy described on page 54. In this taxonomy, "passivity" is considered the least mature reaction to a situation of social conflict; "imaginative helping" is considered the most mature. A passive reaction is reflected in a student's decision to take no action. A "passive emotional" reaction is indicated in the answer "Take no action, but feel very resentful." "Adult dependency," a step up the taxonomy, is suggested if the student appeals to the authority of parents or teacher for a solution. On the other hand, a student who turns to the peer group for an answer may be exhibiting "peer dependence." McPhail sees "aggressive" reactions in threats and destructive solutions, yet aggressiveness is placed at a higher level on the taxonomy than dependence and passivity (and no rationale for this rating is given). "Experimental crude" responses seem to represent expedient solutions rather than harmful or just ones. A more subtle and inventive form of expediency is embodied in the category "experimental sophisticated," although McPhail does not distinguish this from the "crude" version in any precise way. Finally, crowning the taxonomy are the mature responses: "mature conventional" and "mature imaginative." Conventional responses show little independent thinking, but they do reveal a basic respect for fair procedure. Unfortunately, it is difficult to discriminate between "adult dependency" and "mature conventional" in many of the examples. "Mature imaginative" is characterized by original and particularly fair and effective solutions to social problems.

McPhail cautions that this taxonomy should not be used as a basis for channeling discussion toward "higher" levels. This is fortunate because the categories are not clearly defined. But there is some utility in the classification system. The system should "help the teacher to recognize the possibilities in a given situation . . . help the teacher to recognize the adolescent's difficulties so as to be in a better position to assist him . . . provide a list of responses that the teacher can use as further subjects for discussion, role play, and so forth in a form where the courses of action suggested have been limited." These general statements of purpose provide few specifics as to how the teacher is to use the taxonomy, however, and thus its relevance remains elusive.

McPhail does suggest a relatively clear sequence of procedures for teaching with the sensitivity cards. Although he encourages teachers to experiment with alternative strategies, he has used the following approach successfully in many classrooms:

1. Read out or write on the board a situation for consideration.
2. Ask the class to write down on a piece of paper what they would do in this situation. (Students who have difficulty expressing their thoughts on paper can be asked to think what they would do.)

3. Ask for suggested courses of action or collect the papers and choose one to start with.
4. Invite a group of students who have made a similar response to role-play the situation, the response, and what they think would happen subsequently. (If they are initially reluctant, invite volunteers or ask them to argue in support of their response and encourage a discussion.)
5. Initiate class criticism of the response and any other aspects of the role play.
6. Continue by inviting the role play and/or discussion of further responses suggested by the students only as long as interest is strongly maintained.
7. Some summing-up by the class and the teacher is in order, but an obvious and emphatic commitment to one response by the teacher during the early stages of this work is not to be encouraged. It is better to discuss the pros and cons of different courses of action and let the students make a final judgment.

UNIT 2: *CONSEQUENCES*

This unit consists of seventy-one situation cards. The situations in *Consequences* differ from those in *Sensitivity* in that they are not dyadic but involve large numbers of people. Work in *Consequences* is intended as a corrective to the tendency to think of morality exclusively in terms of how *A* treats *B*, "which could result from the adolescent's natural concern with himself and his immediate contacts." The situations stimulate the adolescent to think beyond the morality of one-to-one relationships and to take a third-party, or more objective, perspective.

The basic question posed in the consequences cards is "What is likely to happen next?" As in the sensitivity units, cards can be distributed to individuals or groups, selectively or at random, as a stimulus for role-play, mime, creative writing, discussion, artwork, or the basis of a survey in which the students' predictions of consequences are recorded. McPhail reports that most teachers find that students enjoy using these cards with one another independently of the teacher and that, with practice, they enjoy the element of uncertainty that selecting a card at random introduces. Below are examples of "consequence" situations:

Someone tries to get a friend to drink more than he wants to.

Someone buys a puppy without considering whether he can afford to keep it.

Someone drives a car without being insured.

Someone blames minority groups for everything that is wrong with the country.[4]

UNIT 3: POINTS OF VIEW

This unit consolidates and completes the first section of the Lifeline program. The unit encourages students to "take the role of the other" before finally saying what they would do in a particular situation. Sixty-three situations of conflict form the basis of the unit. The situations are arranged under the following headings: sex attitudes; age conflicts; class attitudes; racial, cultural, religious, and political conflicts; and psychological conflicts. The first situation in the sex attitudes category, for example, includes the following information, which appears on a card animated by a vividly colored picture:

Situation 1. *The girl's position.*

I am the only daughter in the family and am trying to take care of the house while my mother is in the hospital. I think that my brother should accept his share of the household jobs, and I have asked him to help with the cleaning and dishes. He has refused because he does not think that these are jobs for a man.

Try to put yourself in the girl's position. What would you do, say, and feel about it? What might be a solution to this situation that would be acceptable to both the brother and the sister?

The boy's position.

My sister is taking care of the house while our mother is in the hospital. She asked me to help with the cleaning and dishes, but I'm not going to because I think that these are a woman's job.

Try to put yourself in the boy's position. What would you do, say, and feel about it? [5]

Proving the Rule

The purpose of *Proving the Rule*, section 2 in the Lifeline program, is to "give young people opportunities to work out solutions to a variety of familiar problems that may arise as they attempt to achieve adult status and live and work on a basis of equality with other adults." The material does not emphasize current moral and social problems, such as drug dependence or irresponsible attitudes toward sex, for McPhail believes that "we should emphasize the positive aspects of our work, not because we think these are unique topics, but because solutions to these problems are implicit in the approach." *Proving the Rule* is thus not in any direct sense a unit in analyzing controversial public issues, although the skills and dispositions the unit tries to develop are relevant to an understanding of critical social problems.

Proving the Rule explores the problems that Paul, a young adolescent, encounters in various social settings—at school, in the home, and on the job. Five booklets or units, each with a different focus, make up this second section and are discussed below.

UNIT 1: RULES AND INDIVIDUALS

This unit consists of a number of short situations concerning conflicts Paul experiences in handling his responsibilities. The themes of the unit are

1. The complexity of the notion of a rule. "Rule" covers laws, regulations, principles, and social rules among others, and these different kinds of rules enter into morality in different ways.

2. The nature and extent of the problems that arise when different rules conflict.
3. The nature and extent of the problems that arise when rules conflict with inclinations.
4. In general, the importance of decisions in morality.

"Paul, a law breaker" is one example of a situation in this unit:

Paul was helping with the school fund drive. It was Wednesday, and he had promised to take Liz to the movies. But he was broke. He was "borrowing" a few dollars from the fund when he was caught redhanded and sent to the principal. The principal called Paul's parents to tell them about the situation and to notify them that he was suspending Paul from school for a week.

Questions

1. Do you think that the principal behaved fairly or unfairly in this situation? What would you have done if you were the principal?
2. How do you think Paul's parents would react to this situation? Do you think they might punish him too? If so, how?
3. Think of some of the rules which people you know have broken, and then say:
   a) If you think the punishment they got was fair.
   b) If not, what you think a fair punishment might have been.
4. What about people who break rules and are not caught? Use the following situations: in school, in a movie theatre, at home.

Things to Do

1. Role-play the dialogue that could have taken place between Paul and the principal.[6]

UNIT 2: *WHAT DO YOU EXPECT?*

This unit is designed to help the adolescent examine more explicitly the norms and structures of adult society. The first part of this two-part unit concerns social and moral expectations; the second part treats legal expectations. In unit 2, students are expected to widen their social perspective from that of the first unit. Laws and institutions, and the concept of society as a whole, take on increasing significance. Conflicts portrayed in *What Do You Expect?* involve, among others, the psychological and legal implications of a father's neglect of his children, the issue of compulsory education and the legal age of adulthood, the rights of students to protect their lockers from unannounced searches, and the options of a worker who is being exploited by his boss. With this material, students discuss relatively sophisticated problems in social relations.

UNIT 3: *WHO DO YOU THINK I AM?*

This booklet deals with issues of person-perception and self-definition. Notions such as stereotyping, scapegoating, idealization of public figures, and communication breakdown are explored. The underlying premise of the unit is that adolescents need to develop secure and reality-based personal concepts if they are to face social issues with integrity. In McPhail's words, the booklet is designed to "help adolescents cope better with conflict situations and conflicting expectations by helping them establish an idea of themselves and other people as significant, unique individuals who affect situations and make real decisions." A lesson on "My Identity" runs this way:

John's friends think of him as a clever person because he is so good at mechanics. John likes to be thought of in this way. He doesn't like school very much, and as a result, doesn't get along with a group of bright kids in his class.

He calls them bookworms.

They say that he's a dummy.

John and this group of students never really talked to each other, because neither admired or respected the other for what each could do well.

John needed to be admired as a good mechanic because this is how he saw himself. The other group needed to be admired for their school work.

Many people seem to pigeonhole others into "types" or "kinds." Of course, people can't be easily labeled like this. If you selected one aspect of a person and used that as a label, it wouldn't tell you much about what kind of person he or she really is. Could anyone put you in a jar marked "teen-ager" and say what kind of person you are?

Questions

1. Write a list of labels you have used for other people.
2. Draw some jars, label them, and try to fit people you know into them.[7]

UNITS 4 AND 5: *IN WHOSE INTERESTS?* AND *WHY SHOULD I?*

These units present the most complex, and the most fact-laden, situations. Unit 4 focuses on group relations. Students are helped to discover the personal and political importance of group activity and to reflect on the conflicts that such activity may generate. Unit 5's central theme is authority—the authority of parents, groups, social rules, media, myths, and science. The overall intent is to demystify the role of authority in the minds of adolescents. Students are helped to examine authority in an informed and objective manner. In one situation in unit 4, "Life in School," a group of high school students decides to take action to get new classrooms and lab facilities. In a segment of unit 5, the authority of media poses the question of the credibility of various forms of reporting and broadcasting. Both units promote critical and systematic thinking.

What Would You Have Done?

In this section, dramatic moments in history provide springboards for moral reflection. There are six booklets in the series, each built around a different set of historical circumstances. *Birth Day* is set in Durban, South Africa, in 1904 and deals with the birth of an African baby in the dispensary of an

American missionary doctor. *Solitary Confinement* is set in England in 1917 and treats the behavior of a conscientious objector in the army and military attitudes toward him. *Arrest!* is set in Amsterdam in 1944 and deals with the discovery and arrest of Anne Frank and her Jewish family, who had been hiding from the German forces occupying Holland. *Street Scene* is set in Los Angeles in 1965 and focuses on an episode (the stopping of a black man for drunken driving) that sparked the Los Angeles riots. *Tragedy, South Vietnam 1966,* has as its main character a fourteen-year-old boy who is in the hospital with serious burns. *Gale in the Hospital* is set in London in 1969 and deals with a teen-age girl who is in the hospital suffering from the aftereffects of drugs. *What Would You Have Done?* can be readily integrated with traditional academic study in history, social studies, and English.

The Lifeline curriculum is, in sum, a relatively comprehensive approach to moral education. The situations move from simple and immediate face-to-face interactions to complex historical problems. The materials can be used on a group or individual basis and lend themselves to a variety of creative activities from essay writing to sociodrama. According to reports from British teachers who have used Lifeline, the curriculum succeeds in engaging student interest and developing social awareness.

SUMMARY AND APPRAISAL

As suggested, McPhail's model is more impressive in practice than in theory. For a more rigorous theoretical treatment, we encourage the reader to consult the Kohlberg, Shaver, and Newmann models. But the shortcomings of McPhail's theory should not blind one to the value of the Lifeline materials. The cards and booklets are attractively designed, the content is lifelike, and the questions are stimulating. Unfortunately, in the absence of a firm theoretical base, the teacher may be unsure of the overall focus and direction of the curriculum.

McPhail's theoretical arguments lack coherence. His analysis of the sources of motivation in moral behavior is particularly fragmented and inconsistent. He argues, for example, that people "are moved or disposed to treat others with consideration for their needs, feelings, and interests without any prior value judgment or premature use of the word *ought*. We are convinced that this happens and that it happens because it is generally pleasant and rewarding to treat another considerately. It takes no study of ethics or morality to recognize that there are rewards in meeting another's needs." Thus, we act morally because it makes us feel good to do so; the moral life is the pleasant life. Virtue is certainly its own reward in the consideration model. Yet McPhail fails to make clear what precisely he means by "pleasure" and on what basis he judges it to be the single most important motivation in moral behavior. Instead of addressing this issue squarely, he notes that, in addition to pleasure, sixteen other factors account for moral motivation. These factors range from the Christian spirit of agape, or unconditional love, to the Freudian idea of superego, to the philosopher Bergson's notion of spontaneous moral striving. But McPhail does little to integrate the sixteen perspectives into a unified whole. His treatment is more a potpourri of conflicting perceptions than a move toward synthesis. He seems to want to have his cake and eat it too—to claim that pleasure is *the* principle of moral motivation, but that all other opposing explanations make sense too.

McPhail has a tendency to hide theoretical inconsistencies behind high-sounding but evasive rhetoric. He argues, for example, that "conditioning" and "programming" are the stock of a teacher's trade. In his view, ". . . every human being is conditioned. . . . All adults interfere with the so-called natural development of the young. We submit that it is better to know what is happening, to acknowledge and understand these influences, than to delude ourselves that we are permitting the child freedom to grow in his or her own way. That is simply a dangerous self-delusion." McPhail thus implies a deterministic and mechanistic conception of human behavior. Yet he also writes that we must help students become "flexible, humanistic," and able to "choose, construct, and develop the society in which they and their children will have to live. . . . Once they lose control of their environment, feeling themselves to be merely the pawns of abstract historical processes or impersonal institutions, then they will experience much difficulty in regarding themselves or others as full bodied individuals."

How is the teacher to condition students to go beyond the contingencies of reinforcement? How can one mold people to be free? Or, from a different angle, why do we need conditioning if moral behavior is its own reward? Notions of freedom and determinism are used uncritically and carelessly. McPhail's attempt at an integration of these notions is reflected in the following passage:

> Another set of fears is sometimes expressed in terms of conditioning or brainwashing students. The work we propose, however, is not dependent on operant conditioning, in the scientific, Skinnerian sense of that much abused word. There are no immediately "right" responses that are rewarded with credits or candy, no "wrong" responses that bring reproaches, much less punishment. What is right or wrong, appropriate or inappropriate, rewarding or frustrating, is determined by the feedback from the class both individually and collectively, not by a white-frocked clinician trying to make his laboratory "rats" conform to a schedule on a sheet of paper in his hand. The rewards are those enjoyed by individuals as a function of their humanity.

If not operant conditioning, what conditioning does he have in mind? And what does he mean when he says that right is determined by the feedback from the class? Does he mean that the majority rules in determining what is morally right? But what if the majority is "peer-dependent" or "aggressive" or "experimental crude," to use McPhail's own terms? Does classroom "feedback" provide the ultimate justification for moral decisions? How is this appeal to the majority linked to the notion that we experience rewards as a function of our humanity? Aren't rewards different for adolescents at different stages of moral development? Would an "aggressive" youngster be rewarded in the same way as a "dependent" one? McPhail leaves us in the dark regarding key aspects of his theory.

We have already pointed out that the categories in McPhail's taxonomy of moral responses are poorly defined. Moreover, there is no explanation of the mechanism by which adolescents move from one stage to the next. If conditioning accounts for development, it is not apparent how this affects the transition from one level of response to the next. Presumably, if conditioning is so powerful a force, teachers could condition youngsters to behave in a mature fashion without waiting for them to pass through the less desirable phases. Yet McPhail argues that adolescence is a time of social experimentation in which students' freedom to try out various roles and identities must be encouraged. Again, it is difficult to find a clear line of reasoning in McPhail's psychological position.

The teacher needs to be especially wary of McPhail's tendency to define moral maturity in terms of the majority ethic. As noted, in his original survey research McPhail equated the norms of a middle-class community with moral maturity. While the *Proving the Rule* series seeks to foster critical and "postconventional" thinking, to borrow a term from Kohlberg's model, original and independent decision making is not sufficiently stressed in McPhail's theoretical writings. And, in the guidelines for teachers, there is no discussion of how to probe student responses to stimulate higher-level thinking. Viewed as a whole, the consideration model seems more concerned with developing conventional responses than autonomous judgment.

The strength of the consideration approach lies in the Lifeline materials. If the teacher can bring to the materials the theoretical insights that other models provide (e.g., Shaver's and Kohlberg's), then the Lifeline program can be a valuable contribution to the enterprise of moral education.

REFERENCES

Principal Source

McPhail, Peter, J. R. Ungoed-Thomas, and Hilary Chapman. *Lifeline*. Niles, Ill.: Argus Communications, 1975.

This kit contains three components: *In Other People's Shoes, Proving the Rule,* and *What Would You Have Done?*, as well as a teacher's guide entitled *Learning to Care*. Much of the material is presented on large colored work cards that lend themselves to discussion of the open-ended situations. Although designed for grades 7–12, some of the material can be used with younger students. *Learning to Care* outlines the rationale for the Lifeline program, describes the program in detail, and discusses how the teacher can implement it.

Related Readings

Erikson, Erik H. *Identity: Youth and Crisis*. New York: Norton, 1968.

Flavell, J. H. *The Development of Role Taking and Communication Skills in Children*. New York: Wiley, 1968.

Kaye, B., and I. Rogers. *Group Work in Secondary Schools*. London: Oxford University Press, 1968.

Shaftel, Fannie, and George Shaftel. *Role Playing for Social Values: Decision Making in the Social Studies*. Englewood Cliffs, N.J.: Prentice-Hall, 1967.

5

A VALUING PROCESS AND CLARIFICATION MODEL

Living in a democracy maximizes a person's opportunities for making choices. The choices an individual makes reflect personal values and in turn help determine those values. Values clarification attempts to help the individual decide what to value. Values clarification advocates point out that within "value-rich" areas such as politics, religion, friendship, love, sex, race, and money, decision making is subject to many influences. Students are exposed to parental, peer, school, and religious influences, which often contradict one another. The effects of such variables as working parents, broken homes, television, big schools, different teachers, a variety of friends, and travel often result in value confusion. The function of schooling in particular, as it relates to values education, is also confused. As schools have become more geographically consolidated, they have moved from teaching the uniform values of a small community to teaching for no values in particular, emphasizing the acquisition of knowledge. But the school continues to teach values through its unstated or "hidden" curriculum. Too often, what is learned is obedience to authority and the awareness that adult models often do not conform to their own values and moral admonitions.

In response to these problems, Louis Raths, Merrill Harmin, and Sidney Simon have developed a model for values education called values clarification. The model is an attempt to help people decrease value confusion and promote a consistent set of values through a *valuing process*.

Underlying this process is the need to avoid indoctrination of views and promote the use of reason in the determination of values. The values clarification process is designed to promote intelligent value choices through a process of choosing, prizing, and behaving.

Values clarification has four key elements:

1. *A focus on life.* Values clarification focuses on relevant life issues. It asks students to focus on their life style and how their personal priorities reflect a hierarchy of values.
2. *Acceptance of what is.* It is important to indicate to students a nonjudgmental acceptance of their value position. This does not necessarily mean that we communicate approval of what someone says or does. This acceptance is meant to assist students in accepting themselves as individuals and in being honest with themselves.
3. *An invitation to reflect further.* Values clarification calls not only for acceptance but also for reflection on values. This is done through (a) "more informed choices, (b) more aware-ness of what it is a person prizes and cherishes, and (c) better integration of choices and prizings into day-to-day be-havior." [1]
4. *A nourishment of personal powers.* Proponents of values clarification hold that as individuals engage in values clarifi-cation, they can gain a sense of personal direction and fulfillment.

THEORY

The values clarification model derives from an analysis of the relationship between values and behavior. "We have found that several kinds of problems children often exhibit in school and at home are profitably seen as caused by values, or more precisely, by a lack of values." [2] Extending this supposition, the theory suggests that how clearly we see ourselves in relationship to society will determine the behavior we will exhibit. Kirschenbaum emphasizes this point in his attempt to clarify the theory:

> A concern for the *consequences* of one's position—both personal and social—has always been central to the clarifying process. From the beginning, value clarification has never encouraged a static "clarity", instead, it is the *ongoing development* of one's values, including actions taken on them, that is valued.[3]

Values clarification theorists believe that those who are clear about what the relationship is between themselves and society most often exhibit the qualities of being positive, purposeful, enthusiastic, proud, and consistent. Those who are confused exhibit tendencies to be apathetic, flighty, uncertain, inconsistent, drifting, overconforming, overdissenting, and role playing. Such confusion about values is not surprising in a complex democratic society constantly experiencing "future shock." But we do not have to accept a confused condition. The values clarification model is an attempt to provide an educational solution—a valuing process that can be taught—that will reduce the behavioral symptoms of value confusion.

What Are Values?

Values emanate from social experience. People are constantly searching for and learning guides to behavior; these guides tend to give focus to life and are called *values*. One of the aims of values clarification is to help people obtain values that will enable them to relate to their ever-changing world in a satisfying and intelligent way. As such, values are not fixed positions or eternal truths. Rather, they are guides grounded in an individual's personal and social experiences.

> We therefore see values as being constantly related to the experiences that shape them and test them. For any one person, they are not so much hard and fast verities as they are the results of hammer-

ing out a style of life in a certain set of surroundings. After a sufficient amount of hammering, certain patterns of evaluating and behaving tend to develop. Certain things are treated as right, desirable, or worthy. These become our values.[4]

The values clarification model is not concerned so much with
what a person believes as with *how* he or she believes.

We therefore cannot be certain what values, what style of life, would
be most suitable for any person. We do, however, have some ideas
about what *processes* might be most effective for obtaining values.[5]

The Valuing Process

To arrive at our own values, we must engage in the process of
choosing, *prizing*, and *acting* on those values. The overall values
clarifying process actually involves seven subprocesses:

Choosing: (1) freely, (2) from alternatives, and (3) after
thoughtful consideration of the consequences of each alternative.
Prizing: (4) cherishing, being happy with the choice; (5) willing to affirm the choice publicly.
Acting: (6) doing something with the choice (7) repeatedly, in
some pattern of life.[6]

An explication of the seven subprocesses might proceed as
follows:

1. *Choosing freely.* There is little likelihood that an individual
   who is forced to adopt a particular value will integrate that
   value into his or her value structure.
2. *Choosing from alternatives.* This is closely related to the first
   subprocess. Making a number of choices available to the
   individual increases the chance that the individual can
   choose freely.
3. *Choosing after considering the consequences.* Valuing is a
   thoughtful process in which the individual attempts consciously to reflect on what will happen if he or she chooses a

particular value. Choosing impulsively will not lead to an intelligent value system.

4. *Prizing and cherishing.* According to Raths, we should cherish our values and consider them an integral aspect of our existence. We should be proud of our values.

5. *Affirming.* If we have chosen our values freely after considering the consequences, then we should be willing to affirm these values. We should not be ashamed of our values but should be willing to share them when the occasion arises.

6. *Acting upon choices.* The values we hold should be apparent from our actions. In fact, our activities should reflect the values we cherish.

7. *Repeating.* If we act on our values, we should do so in a consistent and repetitive pattern. If our actions are inconsistent with our values, then we should examine more closely the relationship between our values and actions.

The valuing process is applied to three kinds of content. First, there are those aspects of a person's life that are called values indicators (e.g., goals or aspirations). Thus, discussion can focus on clarifying the concerns and aspirations of students. Another source of content are personal issues that we face. These include questions about love, friendship, sexuality, work, marriage, and loyalty. Finally, some social issues can be examined through values clarification. Such issues as poverty in communities, racism, freedom of speech, and the right to strike can be subjected to the values clarification process.

One problem with applying the seven subprocesses is the lack of specific criteria. How many alternatives must be available? How often must action be repeated? What is to be considered "thoughtful" in considering consequences? Recognizing this, Kirschenbaum has expanded the values clarifying process by surrounding it with five dimensions: thinking, feeling, choosing, communicating, and acting.

Thinking and feeling had been a major concern prior to Kirschenbaum's expansion of the model. In general, values clarification is the application of critical thinking skills to the affective domain. Kirschenbaum, in explaining the cognitive and affective dimensions, stresses the need for critical thinking, divergent thinking, and moral reasoning. At the same time he emphasizes the need for the development of a mature self-concept under the dimension of feeling.

The values clarifying process, Kirschenbaum points out, necessarily involves social discourse, *communication*. Sharing thoughts and feelings with others is a critical demand of the model. Hence students must also become skilled in listening and conflict resolution skills. The choosing and acting dimensions posited by Kirschenbaum are similar to those subprocesses incorporated in the original seven.

PRACTICE

Essentially the values clarification model is rooted in classroom dialogue. The approach does not aim to instill particular values; rather, the goal is to help students utilize the seven subprocesses of valuing in their own lives and apply these valuing processes to existing and emergent beliefs and behavior.

To accomplish this task the teacher utilizes specifically designed techniques or exercises developed to help students clarify their values according to the criteria specified in each of the seven subprocesses. The teacher and students are aided in this process by recognition of *value indicators*. Value indicators are perhaps too broad to be considered values (i.e., able to meet all seven criteria), but are entities from which values may eventually emerge. Raths, Harmin, and Simon list eight value indicators as examples: (1) goals or purposes, (2) aspirations, (3) attitudes, (4) interests, (5) feelings, (6) beliefs and convictions, (7) activities, (8) worries, problems and obstacles.

Goals or purposes are usually value indicators because they indicate general directions. Nevertheless, goals or purposes can be explored with the student to see whether the seven processes can be applied to develop values. Typical keywords that signal the statement of purposes are

We're thinking about doing . . .
On the fifteenth, I'm going . . .

On the way downtown we're . . .
I wrote for the plans . . .
When I get this . . . I'm going to do that . . .
We're waiting to hear from him . . .
Boy! Will Saturday ever come?
I'd like to . . .[7]

Aspirations can indicate possible long-term commitments. Again the teacher can assist the student in examining the depth of these commitments through the seven criteria of valuing. Typical keywords that signal the statement of aspirations:

In the future . . .
When I grow up . . .
Someday, I'm going to . . .
My long-range plan is . . .
In about ten years I'm . . .
If all goes well . . .
One of these days . . .[8]

Attitudes. Sometimes we may be for or against something, and this usually represents an attitude toward something. Typical keywords that signal the statement of attitudes:

I'm for . . .
I'm against . . .
I feel that . . .
I think if . . .
The way I see it . . .
If you ask me . . .
In my opinion . . .
My choice is . . .
My way of doing it is . . .
I'm convinced that . . .
I believe . . .[9]

Interests represent a more casual attitude toward something. Interests can indicate general direction but rarely qualify as values. Typical keywords in the statement about activities:

I love making (or doing) . . .
My hobby is . . .
Yes, I subscribe to . . .
I really enjoy reading about . . .
If I had my choice I'd take the ticket to . . .
Most weekends I'm over at the . . .
Every night after school I . . .
Boy, nothing makes me feel better than . . .
I got this catalogue on . . .[10]

Feelings reflect passing emotions that may or may not reflect deeper value commitments. Feelings need to be examined with the seven criteria in order to see if they represent values. Typical keywords that signal a statement involving feelings:

I'd feel bad if . . .
I got angry when . . .
I heard good news about . . .
I had a hard time when . . .
Listen to what Sally did . . .
I would like . . .
I feel guilty when . . .[11]

Beliefs and convictions. On the surface, beliefs may seem to be values, but often the person may not prize the belief or may not have freely chosen the belief. Thus it is not necessarily a value.

Activities may also represent values. Only on examination, however, can we ascertain whether activities reflect basic values. For example, a person may go to church but this attendance may not be out of individual choice. Thus, activities may or may not indicate a value. Typical keywords that signal a statement about activities:

After school, I usually . . .
Last weekend, we . . .
On my day off, I went . . .
One of the best things we did Halloween . . .
. . . all yesterday afternoon.
We just like to play . . .[12]

Worries, problems, obstacles. These indicate concerns but usually do not represent well-developed values.

Value indicators are often revealed in common classroom discourse and are clues to what students believe they value. Providing students with opportunities to reveal these value indicators is part of the environment that needs to be created and is the purpose of the techniques and strategies provided by values clarifying adherents.

Clarifying Responses

Because the values clarification process involves discussion, teachers must be careful not to impose their value system as the "right" answer. An atmosphere in which all feel respected, trusted, and free to either speak or remain silent and listen to others is a requirement. Participants must recognize that *accepting* the thoughts or feelings of another does not imply *agreement*. The clarifying process is a voluntary endeavor and respects the privacy of each individual.

The purpose of the values clarifying strategies is to create a nonthreatening dialogue. The dialogue is "soft," meaning that confrontation or constant probing is unwarranted. Unlike discussion and dialogue in other models, such as Kohlberg's discussion, here it is desired to be "permissive and stimulating, but not insistent."

A good example of this dialogue is demonstrated in the "clarifying responses" that undergird all other values clarification classroom techniques. This responding strategy is meant to delicately stimulate thinking about one's own values. Here are examples of clarifying questions.

Clarifying Responses Suggested by the Seven Valuing Processes

1. *Choosing freely*
   a. Where do you suppose you first got that idea?
   b. How long have you felt that way?
   c. What would people say if you weren't to do what you say you must do?

    d. Are you getting help from anyone? Do you need more help? Can I help?

    e. Are you the only one in your crowd who feels this way? . . .

2. *Choosing from alternatives*
   a. What else did you consider before you picked this?
   b. How long did you look around before you decided?
   c. Was it a hard decision? What went into the final decision? Who helped? Do you need any further help?
   d. Did you consider another possible alternative?
   e. Are there some reasons behind your choice? . . .

3. *Choosing thoughtfully and reflectively*
   a. What would be the consequences of each alternative available?
   b. Have you thought about this very much? How did your thinking go?
   c. Is this what I understand you to say . . . (interpret statement)?
   d. Are you implying that . . . (distort statement to see if the student is clear enough to correct the distortion)?
   e. What assumptions are involved in your choice? Let's examine them. . . .

4. *Prizing and cherishing*
   a. Are you glad you feel that way?
   b. How long have you wanted it?
   c. What good is it? What purpose does it serve? Why is it important to you?
   d. Should everyone do it your way? . . .

5. *Affirming*
   a. Would you tell the class the way you feel some time?
   b. Would you be willing to sign a petition supporting that idea?
   c. Are you saying that you believe . . . (repeat the idea)?
   d. You don't mean to say that you believe . . . (repeat the idea)?

    e. Should a person who believes the way you do speak out? . . .

6. *Acting upon choices*
    a. I hear what you are for; now, is there anything you can do about it? Can I help?
    b. What are your first steps, second steps, etc.?
    c. Are you willing to put some of your money behind this idea?
    d. Have you examined the consequences of your act?
    e. Are there any organizations set up for the same purposes? Will you join? . . .

7. *Repeating*
    a. Have you felt this way for some time?
    b. Have you done anything already? Do you do this often?
    c. What are your plans for doing more of it?
    d. Should you get other people interested and involved?
    e. Has it been worth the time and money? . . .[13]

Clarifying responses are characterized by the following elements:

1. Clarifying responses avoid moralizing or focusing on "right" or "wrong" responses.
2. Their purpose is to put responsibility on the students to decide for themselves.
3. The clarifying response does not always expect the student to respond and allows him or her to "pass."
4. The goal of the clarifying response is very limited. It does not aim at changing behavior but at setting a mood.
5. Clarifying responses are not used to interview students but to stimulate thought.
6. Extended discussion does not usually result from a clarifying response but only in short dialogue. In fact, the teacher usually breaks off the conversation with "nice talking to you," etc.
7. Clarifying responses are aimed at individuals. They are most useful in one-to-one encounters rather than in group discussion.

8. The teacher does not respond to everything everyone says or does in a classroom.
9. Clarifying responses do not attempt to move the student toward a "right" answer. They do not involve questions that move the student toward an answer the teacher has in mind.
10. There are no set patterns to clarifying responses. They should arise naturally in the course of the conversation and not be used in a mechanical way.[14]

Here is an example of a teacher using a clarifying response:

T.: What exactly do you like about science?
S.: Specifically? Let me see. Gosh, I'm not sure. I guess I just like it in general.
T.: Do you do anything outside of school to have fun with science?
S.: No, not really.
T.: Thank you, Lise. I must get back to work now.[15]

The clarifying response technique is essentially a one-to-one dialogue.

Values sheets are another possible strategy. Raths suggests that students *write* their own responses to the sheets. Informal discussion can follow but the emphasis in the values sheet is on writing and personal reflection. If discussion is employed with the values sheets, Raths suggests that small groups of students be used rather than large-group discussion, which tends to be more threatening. Below is a values sheet.

Values Sheet 9. *On Civil Liberties*

The National Defense Education Act of 1958 stipulated that a student wanting a federal loan for education purposes had to sign an affidavit stating that he "does not believe in, and is not a member of and does not support any organization that believes in or teaches, the overthrow of the United States Government by force or violence or by any illegal or uncon-stitutional methods."

1. What do you think of such a requirement? (Check one.)
   _____ Seems reasonable. I would not mind signing such an affidavit.
   _____ Seems unreasonable, but not seriously so. Not worth making a fuss over.
   _____ Seems unreasonable, and seriously so. I would not accept money under such conditions and believe the law should be changed.
   _____ (Any other position; write it out here.)

2. Some persons did think such a "loyalty oath" serious and refused to accept money on that basis. In fact, some thirty-two of the nation's leading colleges and universities had officially notified the Office of Education that they had withdrawn from or declined to participate in the program specifically because of that requirement. Another sixty-three institutions participated, but under protest.
   Why do you think some schools protested that oath?

3. The provision was repealed by Congress in the 1962 session. President Kennedy said when he signed the repeal that the oath was "offensive" to college students.
   Under what conditions do you think the government should change laws when the people object?

4. Discuss your feelings about this matter further. Perhaps you will want to discuss the general relationship between citizens and government, or what you would have done in the specific situation described above, or what you will do in the future under such circumstances.[16]

Finally, there are strategies that can involve large-group discussion. For example, the values continuum strategy might involve the entire class.

Purpose

The values continuum serves to open up the range of alternatives possible on any given issue. Students begin to realize that on most issues there are many shades of gray, and they are more likely to move away from the either-or, black-white thinking which often occurs when controversial issues are discussed in the classroom. The continuum also encourages students to make a public affirmation of their opinions and beliefs.

Procedure

An issue is identified by either the teacher or the class. This issue may have presented itself during a class discussion or it may have been prepared beforehand by the teacher. We will use as an example the issue of government economic controls—often thought of as socialism versus capitalism.

The teacher draws a long line on the board, and he, or he and the class, determine two polar positions on the issue. For example, one end position might be "Complete government control over economic affairs," and the other end position might be "Absolutely no government control over the economic system." The two positions are placed on the opposite ends of the line, as shown below.

Complete   No
control .... control

The teacher then marks a series of points along the continuum, saying, "Between these end points there are numerous other positions. I am going to whip around the room and ask you to tell me where you stand on this issue. Briefly describe your position, without giving your reasons for holding that position. Tell me how much control you think is desirable and indicate where along the continuum you want to place yourself. Later you can share your reasons for your position. You may pass if you wish."

The teacher goes around the room or calls on volunteers.

The students place their names on the line and briefly tell what their placement stands for. If five to ten students respond, this is usually enough to get a spread of opinion and to give everyone time to determine his own position. The teacher may then put his own name on the line and explain what his position is, or he, too, may pass.

By now every student in the room has considered the issue for himself, and a free-wheeling discussion easily begins.[17]

With discussion strategies, a four-step process can be used. First, a topic is selected. Some ways to initiate discussion include using quotations, pictures without captions, a scene from a play or movie, and provocative questions. Second, the students should have an opportunity to think before talking. This can sometimes be accomplished by having students write down their responses to the strategy or question. Third, the class can discuss the question in small groups or as a whole group. Small groups can be utilized for an initial short period, then the class can meet as a whole. Finally, the students can sit and reflect on the experience through such questions as

I learned that . . .
I discovered that . . .
I am beginning to wonder . . .
I was surprised . . .[18]

VALUES VOTING

Here the teacher surveys the class to see how different individuals feel about values issues. It also allows students to publicly affirm their values.

The teacher reads aloud a question, and the students can vote on the issue by raising their hands in the affirmative or pointing their thumbs down to indicate disagreement. Undecided students can fold their arms. Some questions that can be used include these: How many of you

1. think teen-agers should be allowed to choose their own clothes?
2. will raise your children more strictly than you were raised?
3. watch TV more than three hours per day?
4. think the most-qualified person usually wins in school elections?
5. think there are times when cheating is justified?

6. could tell someone they had bad breath?
7. think going steady is important in order to achieve social success?
8. regularly attend religious services and enjoy it? [19]

RANK ORDER

This strategy asks students to choose values from competing choices and then affirm their values. After the students have completed these rank-order questions, the choices can be discussed in small groups or with the class as a whole. Some sample rank-order questions include

1. Where would you rather be on a Saturday afternoon?
   _____ at the beach
   _____ in the woods
   _____ in a discount store
2. How do you learn best?
   _____ through lectures
   _____ through independent study
   _____ through seminars
3. Which would you give the lowest priority to today?
   _____ space
   _____ poverty
   _____ defense
   _____ ecology [20]

EITHER-OR FORCED CHOICE

Here the student chooses between two alternatives. If the teacher wishes, he or she can place the alternatives on either side of the room and then the students can move to the side of the room that represents their view. Some sample either-or forced choices include the following:

Are you
_____ 1. more of a saver or a spender?
_____ 2. more like New York City or Colorado?
_____ 3. more of a loner or a grouper?

_____ **4.** more like a rose or a daisy?
_____ **5.** more like breakfast or dinner?
_____ **6.** more like summer or winter? [21]

VALUES FOCUS GAME

Some of the values clarification strategies focus on listening skills. This strategy asks the student to respond to a stem sentence such as "I feel best when I am in a group of people that. . . ." Then triads are formed and each student is to have the full attention of the two others in the group for five minutes. Three rules are important to this process.

1. *The rule of focusing.* Each group member is to be the focus person for a period of five minutes. Do not let the attention of the group shift from the focus person until his time is up or until he asks to stop. Maintain eye contact with the focus person at a comfortable level. Questions may be asked of the focus person if they do not shift the focus to another group member.
2. *The rule of acceptance.* Be warm, supportive, and accepting of the focus person. Nods, smiles, and expressions of understanding when sincerely given help communicate acceptance. If you do not agree with the focus person, do not express disagreement or negative feelings during the discussion part of the game. There will be time for this later on.
3. *The rule of drawing out.* Attempt to understand the focus person's position, feelings, and beliefs. Ask questions that will help to clarify the reasons for the focus person's feelings. Make sure that your questions do not shift the focus to yourself, or reveal negative feelings you may have about the focus person or about what he is saying. [22]

UNFINISHED SENTENCES

The strategy helps students explore certain attitudes, goals, etc. What sometimes emerges from this activity is an awareness of developing values. Some sentences that can be completed include

1. On Saturdays, I like to . . .
2. If I had 24 hours to live . . .
3. If I had my own car . . .
4. I feel best when people . . .
5. If I had a million dollars, I would . . .
6. Secretly I wish . . .
7. My children won't have to . . .[23]

The teacher then whips around the room asking students to complete their sentences out loud. Students are free to pass.

RESEARCH

Values clarification proponents have accumulated some research evidence and claim that values clarification can lead to

- A reduction in the intensity and/or frequency of the eight unclear behavior patterns
- A reduction in some forms of deviant or disruptive behavior (such as drug use and uncooperative classroom acts)
- An increase in self-direction and trust in oneself (including more self-acceptance)
- A maturation of expressed values (a shift away from values generally judged immature and toward these generally judged more mature)
- An improvement in the learning climate (more participation, more responsibility for what happens, more interest in learning)
- An improvement in social relationships (more friends, greater group cohesion, more empathy for others)
- An improvement in learning outcomes (especially in reading and in learnings on the level of life applications)
- A venting of personal pressures (expressing problems, venting fears)
- An increase in hope and faith (more confidence that problems can be solved, progress is possible, personal power can be marshaled)
- An improvement in student-teacher relations (more feeling

on the part of students that teachers are helpful and kind; more feeling on the part of teachers that students are worthy of respect and affection) [24]

Recognizing the inherent difficulty in designing research studies and problems of adequate measurement, values clarifiers provide summaries of studies that they believe support their theory's contentions.

In 1977 Kirschenbaum reviewed nineteen studies that he believed tended to support values clarification. Generally speaking, Kirschenbaum's review lends weight in a testimonial sense to the worth of the values clarification theory in action. Nevertheless, most of the studies he reports are at best vague in their results and lack the sophistication and statistically significant results required by most researchers. A similar review is included in the 1978 edition of *Values and Teaching*.

Raths, Harmin, and Simon also suggest that teachers engage in their own informal research. For example, students can be rated according to value-related behaviors. Children can be measured according to their apathy, flightiness, etc., to see if values clarification improves their sense of purpose and integration. A chart can be used to make the assessments. This chart can be filled out at the beginning of the year and then at the end of the year after using a values clarification program. A control group may also be employed. There is still the danger, however, of teacher expectations affecting this assessment.

SUMMARY AND APPRAISAL

While much has been written about values clarification in the past twelve years, the basic tenets of the theory have remained intact. They are perhaps best summarized in *Values and Teaching:*

> We believe that each person has to wrest personal values from the available array. As is elaborated later, values that actually penetrate living in intelligent and consistent ways are not likely to be produced in any other way. Thus it is the process of making such decisions that concerns us. "Instead of giving young people the

Figure 5.1. Form for Measuring the Degree of Value-Related Behavior Problems

Student's name _____

Directions: Please rate the above student on the frequency and acuteness with which he or she exhibits each of the eight types of behaviors listed below. Use the scale provided for your ratings. An elaboration of the meaning of each type of behavior is available if you would like.

Apathy   frequency this student exhibits this trait _____
                acuteness of this behavior for this student _____

Flightiness: frequency _____   *Frequency Scale*
                acuteness _____   0—Never
Uncertainty: frequency _____   1—Almost never
                acuteness _____   2—Perhaps every few months
Inconsistency: frequency _____   3—Monthly, on the average
                acuteness _____   4—Several times monthly
                                        5—Weekly
                                        6—Several times weekly
                                        7—Daily
                                        8—Several times daily
                                        9—Hourly
Drifting: frequency _____   10—Constantly
                acuteness _____
Conformity: frequency _____   *Acuteness Scale*
                acuteness _____
Dissension: frequency _____   0—Not at all
                acuteness _____   1—Extremely mild
Role Playing: frequency _____   2—Mild
                acuteness _____   3—Medium
                                        4—Relatively acute
                                        5—Acute
                                        6—Extremely acute

Source: Louis E. Raths, Merrill Harmin, and Sidney B. Simon, *Values and Teaching* (2nd ed.; Columbus, Ohio: Charles E. Merrill, 1978), p. 276.

impression that their task is to stand a dreary watch over the ancient values," says John Gardner (1964), "we should be telling them the grim but bracing truth that it is their task to recreate those values continuously in their own time." Giving students a process of valuing is giving them something that should serve them well and long. . . .

There is an assumption in our value theory and the teaching strategies that grow from it that humans can arrive at values by an intelligent process of choosing, prizing, and behaving. At least we assume that humans can arrive at something via that process, and with some support in the literature, we prefer to call that something "values."

That assumption (which may seem essentially semantic) need not unduly bother the practical-minded classroom teacher, however, in operation the assumption is transformed into a hypothesis of a different order. If children are helped to use the valuing process of this book, we assert that they will behave in ways that are less apathetic, confused, and irrational and in ways that are more positive, purposeful, and enthusiastic. This hypothesis is readily testable by anyone who wishes to do so.[25]

Values clarification theory is not without its problems. While its acceptance and use has expanded widely over the past decade, so too has the criticism. Such criticism usually falls into one of two related categories: (1) the distinction between moral and nonmoral values, and (2) the problem of values and ethical relativism.

First is the problem of defining a value as something that meets the criteria of the seven-step valuing process. What criteria in each step might prescribe appropriate action? Two examples of this problem are proposed by Lockwood. Both pro- and anti-abortion forces claim to value life. Can the proponents of each side, advocating contradictory behavior, both lay claim to valuing life? Similarly, during the recent Vietnam war, could both the advocates and opponents of bombing North Vietnam claim to value peace? If the answer in these two cases is yes, then we find the criteria for values to be arbitrary in helping one decide how to act.

> The values clarification theory of values would thus be in a position of asserting the same value can support mutually contradictory actions. Such an assertion would appear to vitiate one of the fundamental objectives of values clarification—developing values which provide a clear and consistent guide to behavior.[26]

Hence, although the theory may be successful in helping an individual initially become aware of values issues, it raises value conflicts. Because values clarifiers emphasize individual and personal concerns (interests, tastes, likes), the problem of value conflict within the theory has not been well addressed. Yet the paradox of the theory is that it not only helps clarify certain values well but also causes increased confusion when it is obvious that "clarified values" can conflict, within oneself and between persons. At that point the theory provides little conflict-clarification guidance. But values clarification adherents wish to provide a process that helps determine values guides for our lives. Ironically, values clarification theory, while rooted in the rationale that complex society brings with it a confusion of valuing, may contribute further confusion. Such issues as racism, war, poverty, and human rights attest to value conflict and demand resolution. Left with ethical relativism, people can use their authority and power conspicuously.

For example, consider the teacher who raises the problem of whether cheating is acceptable on tests. Some students may indicate that they think it is acceptable to cheat. But this may conflict with the rules the teacher has established for the class. The teacher using values clarification must be careful, then, as to what is opened to the valuing process. If the teacher opens the cheating issue to discussion, and the students decide it is all right to cheat, then the teacher must either accept that position or resort to the use of power and insist that cheating will not occur within his or her class. If many conflicts arise between the open process of valuing and the position of the teacher, the students may see the valuing process as a "game" and unrelated to real issues that can arise in schools. The teacher may have to limit the issues to be addressed in the classroom if they fundamentally conflict with his or her conception of how things should be run. Otherwise, the teacher will end up having to use authority arbitrarily, which runs counter to the basic ethic of values clarification.

These criteria severely limit teachers to values issues that are fairly safe and bland, thus probably minimizing conflict. Moreover, the criteria pose a new problem for students since the criteria of "reasonable extent" and "distasteful" or "dangerous" will be viewed differently by each teacher, thereby reinforcing the belief that values are relative. Lockwood laments this tendency toward the promotion of relativism in the clarification model.

First, a program of values education which devotes its attention to questions of personal preference and desire represents a truncated

and myopic view of morality. A program which avoids the controversies associated with value conflict, conflict resolution, and
moral justification, trivializes the complexity of value issues in
human affairs. Second, a values education program which, perhaps,
unwittingly, is grounded in ethical relativism must accept the possibility that its students will embrace ethical relativism as their
moral point of view—clearly an achievement of dubious merit. [27]

The moral dimension mentioned above relates to the lack of
distinction between moral and nonmoral values in values
clarification theory. Nonmoral and moral issues are equivalent
issues. Take, for example, some questions asked in the values
voting technique: "How many of you (1) watch your weight, (2)
would like a part-time job, or (3) would encourage legal abortion?" Each relates to preference, but only the third involves a
moral question.

The use of "would" also indicates a confusion between a
concern for "is" and "ought" in moral issues. "Ought" questions, or questions of what you should do, usually relate to
moral concerns. Not that all "should" questions define moral
issues. Clearly, "Should you watch your weight?" may entail an
appearance or medical concern but not a moral issue. Most of
the values clarifying techniques focus on the "would" or "is"
condition. In the values sheet strategy, the instructions to the
student are "Read each of the eight situations below and try to
identify what you would do in each case." [28]

This lack of concern for, or understanding of, the moral
dimension—the consideration of justification for obligatory
behavior—is further reinforced in the admonition that teachers
not ask "why" questions. "Why" questions ask for the grounds
or reasons underlying a belief (its moral foundation), but values
clarification does not negate such questions for that reason.
Rather, it is concerned that students who have no clear reasons
for choices might make up reasons for the benefit of the teacher
and to conform to peer expectations. This seems to contradict
the admonition to trust and respect the views of your students.

The values clarification approach does seem to promote increased awareness of, and sensitivity to, values issues, especially those in the nonmoral domain. The techniques and

strategies it provides seem to evoke student response and can result in a more pleasant, humane, and relevant classroom. While the theory seems to have inherent contradictions and is limited in its definition of values and morality, it can be seen as at least a good starting point for raising important personal and societal concerns. It also has been a popular approach with teachers because the gamelike strategies are easy to use in the classroom and help create a more relaxed and open climate. Without too much modification, a teacher can easily focus more on value conflict and the moral dimensions of such conflict after issues have been raised.

REFERENCES

Principal Sources

Harmin, Merrill, et al. *Clarifying Values Through Subject Matter: Applications for the Classroom*. Minneapolis, Minn.: Winston, 1973.
Explanation of how values clarification can be related to other subject areas including social studies, biology, earth science, mathematics, health, art, and music.

Kirschenbaum, Howard. *Advanced Values Clarification*. La Jolla, Calif.: University Associates, 1977.
Kirschenbaum responds to some of the criticism of values clarification. Also included are suggestions for teacher-training workshops in values clarification.

Raths, Louis E., et al. *Values and Teaching: Working with Values in the Classroom*. Columbus, Ohio: Merrill, 1978.
This is the second edition of the first text on values clarification. It contains theory as well as guidelines for using the approach in the classroom.

Simon, Sidney, et al. *Values Clarification: A Handbook of Practical Strategies for Teachers and Students*. New York: Hart, 1972.
This is a popular text with teachers and contains 79 values clarification strategies that can be used at the elementary and secondary level.

Related Readings

Curwin, Gerre, and Richard Curwin. *Search for Values*. Dayton, Ohio: Pflaum/Standard, 1972.
A set of values clarification activities organized according to various themes (e.g., competition) and intended for grades 9–12.

Elder, Carl. *Making Values Judgments: Decisions for Today*. Columbus, Ohio: Merrill, 1972.

This book focuses on such problems as drugs, race relations, and crime and is designed for the secondary school student.

Harmin, Merrill. *Making Sense of Our Lives*. Niles, Ill.: Argus Communications, 1974.

For secondary school students, this is a kit of cassettes, posters, and values sheets to facilitate values clarification and communications skills.

Harmin, Merrill. *People Projects*. Menlo Park, Calif.: Addison Wesley, 1973.

For grades 4–8, these cards are designed to initiate student projects that develop creative thought as well as values clarification skills.

Lockwood, Alan. "A Critical View of Values Clarification." In *Moral Education: It Comes with the Territory*, ed. David Purpel and Kevin Ryan. Berkeley, Calif.: McCutchan, 1976.

Raths, Louis E. *Exploring Moral Values*. Pleasantville, N.Y.: Warren Schleat, 1969.

Designed for grades 2–6, this program provides opportunities for students to discuss relevant life situations that facilitate values clarification.

Simon, Sidney B. *Meeting Yourself Halfway: 31 Values Clarifications*. Niles, Ill.: Argus Communications, 1974.

Another collection of values strategies designed for adolescence and adulthood.

6
VALUE ANALYSIS

Value analysis is a close cousin of the rationale building model. Both approaches are concerned with the philosophic underpinnings of values education; both appreciate the centrality of conflict in making decisions about values; both look to reason as the key arbiter of value disputes; and both tend to emphasize controversial public issues. What most readily distinguishes value analysis from rationale building is the former's greater attention to pedagogy. Value analysis lays out a step-by-step procedure for helping students deal with values issues.

Moreover, the value analysis pedagogy develops along different lines from values clarification or the cognitive moral development model. Value analysis is more directly concerned than either of these models with helping students gather and weigh the *facts* involved in value judgments. The consideration, values clarification, and cognitive developmental models also deal with context and consequences, but the value analysis treatment is more explicit and sustained.

A thorough account of value analysis is set forth in *Values Education*, which is the forty-first yearbook of the National Council for the Social Studies.[1] Although the yearbook's conception was developed by a team of educators, philosophers, and psychologists including Jerrold Coombs, Milton Meux, and James Chadwick, for brevity's sake we will refer to the model throughout this chapter as the Coombs approach.

Coombs draws a distinction between a value criterion and a value principle that is unique to this model. It is important to understand this distinction before moving on to considerations of teaching strategy. A value criterion, according to Coombs, ascribes value to some class of conditions. Commonly held criteria include it is wrong to cheat, lie, steal, kill, and hurt other people; and it is good to keep promises, pay debts, and be healthy. Value criteria, Coombs notes, "do not specify the manner in which a certain type of condition is to be rated in all circumstances. They indicate only how the condition is to be rated in the main or other things being equal." [2] For example, the value criterion that lying is wrong is generally acceptable and valid. But lying may at times be right, say, when lying will save someone's life or diminish his suffering. Thus we can admit this standard regarding lying as a value criterion and still realize that, in exceptional circumstances, it may not apply.

Value criteria, Coombs continues, give "valence" to facts. They determine whether the facts uphold positive or negative evaluations. In the case of euthanasia, for example, the value criterion "killing is wrong" gives negative valence to the fact that euthanasia involves killing. This fact thus supports a negative evaluation of euthanasia. Whether the value question is simple or complex hinges on the nature and extent of the relevant facts. If all the facts are uniformly positive or negative in valence, the decision is a fairly simple one to make. It becomes difficult when the relevant facts have conflicting valence, that is, when some facts suggest the value object is good and some facts indicate it is not. Then the evaluator must balance the facts and come to a decision. [3]

An example that Coombs offers will help make this clear. Suppose it is 1970 and an evaluator is trying to decide whether or not the United States should withdraw from the war in Vietnam. He accepts the following facts (*f*) and criteria (*c*):

(*f*) 1. **The war in Vietnam is primarily a civil war.**
(*c*) 1. **One country ought not enter into the civil wars of other countries.**

(f) **2.** U.S. withdrawal would result in a substantially reduced rate of killing.

(c) **2.** It is wrong to kill or to cause a large number of killings.

(f) **3.** U.S. withdrawal would reduce the level of civil strife in the U.S.

(c) **3.** A stable, peaceful society is a good thing.

(f) **4.** U.S. withdrawal would free U.S. resources which could be used to cope with pressing social problems in the U.S.

(c) **4.** It is desirable for a society to have the resources available to handle pressing social problems.

(f) **5.** U.S. withdrawal would result in a repressive, communistic society in South Vietnam.

(c) **5.** Illiberal societies are undesirable and immoral.

(f) **6.** The U.S. has committed itself to defending South Vietnam against takeover by the communists.

(c) **6.** A nation ought to honor its commitments.

(f) **7.** U.S. withdrawal would be construed as a sign of weakness and lack of resolve.

(c) **7.** A nation ought not let others think it is weak or irresolute.[4]

From this compilation, the evaluator might come to the conclusion that the United States should withdraw from the Vietnamese war. The evaluator's judgment, according to Coombs, implies the following *principle:* a nation ought not be involved in a civil war to save a country from a repressive government if that involvement increases the level of killing in the war and diverts the nation's attention from pressing social problems.[5] This complex principle emerged as a product of the decision-making process. It reflects the results of value analysis rather than determining its process. What are brought to the context of value judgments, Coombs argues, are not value principles but value criteria. Each *value criterion* provides the basis for evaluating a particular feature of the value object, giving either positive or negative valence to that feature. The *value principle* applies to the value object as a whole. It is the principle that weighs the claims of the various rival criteria, yet we are aware of the principle only after a value decision has been made and the reasons for it given.

As suggested in chapter 1, Coombs' distinction between a criterion and a principle is similar to Shaver's distinction between a value and a qualified general position. For Shaver, a value is a criterion for appraising the worth or propriety of an object, action, or trait. When we make a complex decision, Shaver stresses, we must balance conflicting values (e.g., stability v. change, work v. play, industry v. ecology). The qualified position we reach is a statement of the way in which our values relate to one another in certain situations. This statement serves the same function as Coombs' notion of principle. Both a "qualified position" and a "principle" spell out the value priorities in a given case.

To return to Coombs' example about the Vietnam war, the principle does not simply state that "a nation ought not to be involved in another nation's civil war"; rather, it asserts that "a nation ought not be involved in a civil war to save a country from a repressive government if that involvement increases the level of killing in the war and diverts the nation's attention from pressing social problems." The criterion, or value, of noninterference is thus not treated as an absolute but as a value that is qualified in application by other important considerations. Presumably, intervention might be justified, according to the principle, if such an action did not increase the level of killing and did not compromise the nation's commitment to improving its domestic welfare. Both a principle, in Coombs' terms, and a qualified position, in Shaver's language, reflect a *system* of values rather than merely a single value statement.

Kohlberg, too, stresses that a moral judgment requires an individual to place in a logical hierarchy various moral beliefs. For example, a person may value both property rights and human life. In a decision in which the violation of property rights leads to the salvation of life (e.g., when someone must rob a store in order to obtain a drug for a critically ill person), the value of life commands a higher priority than the value of property. The values of friendship and honesty, authority and truth, and loyalty and justice may similarly conflict. In order to resolve such conflicts, an individual must see the logical connections among values and recognize which are fundamental and which are derivative. To Kohlberg, moral principles enable people to accomplish such value ordering in a consistent way. This is one reason why "principled moral reasoning" is considered more "adequate" than rule-oriented or self-interested forms of judgment.

A STRATEGY FOR TEACHING VALUE ANALYSIS AND VALUE CONFLICT RESOLUTION

There are six essential procedures in value analysis. They form the basis of, and are parallel to, the six tasks of the conflict resolution sequence: [6]

Value Analysis Tasks	*Conflict Resolution Tasks*
1. Identifying and clarifying the value question	1. Reducing differences in the interpretation of the value question
2. Assembling purported facts	2. Reducing differences in the purported facts assembled
3. Assessing the truth of purported facts	3. Reducing differences in the assessed truth of purported facts
4. Clarifying the relevance of facts	4. Reducing differences in the relevance of facts
5. Arriving at a tentative value decision	5. Reducing differences in tentative value decisions
6. Testing the value principle implied in the decision	6. Reducing differences in testing the acceptability of value principles

Although the two strategies are parallel, we present each of them separately in this chapter.

Value Analysis Tasks

1. *Identifying and clarifying the value question.* Value questions are often stated in vague or ambiguous terms. Such confusion

may result for at least two reasons. First, the point of view from which the judgment is to be made may be unclear. For example, in the question "Should students take over university buildings to call attention to their grievances?" it is not clear whether we are being asked to evaluate the proposed action from the viewpoint of effectiveness or from a moral point of view. Second, the value object we are being asked to judge may not be clearly specified. For example, consider the question "Is it all right to use drugs?" We don't know whether to focus on a particular drug or drugs in general. When students do not know precisely what they are evaluating or from what standpoint they are to make the evaluation, deliberation tends to be frustrating and unproductive.

Teachers need to clarify the value question and teach students to do the same. A teacher might introduce and clarify a value question about drugs by specifying the moral point of view as the standard of judgment and by defining "drugs" in terms of addictive, consciousness-altering substances. To crystallize the definition even further, the teacher might provide examples of substances that would be considered drugs in this instance and substances that would not be so considered.

At times, the teacher and the students should share the responsibility of clarifying the value question. In these cases, the teacher might probe for an exact definition of the value object and the relevant point of view. The clarification process might also be deliberately delayed so that confusion develops and students see on their own the importance of clarification.

2. Assembling purported facts. Before they set out to gather facts relevant to a value decision, students must be able to distinguish between factual and evaluative statements. Factual statements report or describe observable conditions or events. Evaluative statements rate things with respect to their worth. Evaluative statements are guides to how persons are to act, choose, or feel about something; factual statements do not perform this function. It is a *fact*, for instance, that cars run on gasoline. It is an *evaluation* to say that we should put gas in cars. We cannot justify or verify an evaluation on the basis of observation alone. No matter how much we examine, test, or prod a car, we cannot discover the concept of "should" within its nature. We may decide in the light of our observations that we should fill the car with gas, but we do not observe this.

Once students are clear about the difference between factual and evaluative assertions, they need to learn to assemble a wide range of facts from as many sources as possible. During this phase of fact gathering, the teacher should

1. Have students organize facts around different concerns (e.g., economic, ecological, aesthetic, moral)
2. Have students distinguish facts on the basis of whether they have a positive or negative "valence"
3. Subsume specific facts under more general data
4. Rank facts according to their significance for the value decision [7]

To simplify and systematize this process, the students can develop a chart that organizes the data. A sample chart is shown in figure 6.1.

   3. Assessing the truth of purported facts. Facts relevant to a value decision can be particular facts, general facts, or conditional facts. A particular factual assertion describes a single event or condition, such as "George Washington was the first President of the United States." General facts are generalizations that can be tested empirically by reference to the particular facts that support or refute them. "DDT can kill people" is a general fact, one that can be verified or falsified by observing people who have eaten DDT. Conditional facts (*if-then* assertions) are verified by finding out whether or not anything analogous to the "then" part of the claim has in the past followed the occurrence of things analogous to what is specified in the "if" part of the claim. An example of a conditional fact is "If the auto workers extend their strike for another month, [then] the price of cars next year will certainly rise."

The teacher needs to help students develop a critical posture

Figure 6.1. A Fact-Assembly Chart, with the Value Object "Use of DDT"

	Value Object: Use of DDT				
Basic Concerns	**POSITIVE**		**NEGATIVE**		**Subsidiary Value Judgments**
	General	Specific	General	Specific	
Ecology			DDT gets concentrated in the food chain so that animals and people at the end of the food chain get concent. DDT	Lake Michigan study 0.0085 ppm in sediment 0.41 ppm in tiny invertebrates 3–8 ppm in flesh of fish eating invertebrates 3,177 ppm in fatty tissue of gulls feeding on fish Trillionths in rain and surface water 5–20 ppm in fatty tissues of people	Highly detrimental
			DDT destroys natural controls and balances in pests		

Economic	DDT has a large market DDT costs less than alternative methods of control		DDT costs more than formerly	See decreasing power to kill insects	Much less useful and effective
Practical	DDT is persistent DDT kills a broad range of insects DDT's alternatives cost more and require more ingenuity to find	Resists breakdown by water, microbes, and sunlight Flies, mosquitoes, bollworm Harder marketing methods More specialized controls New research needed	DDT is decreasing in power to kill insects DDT has available alternatives	Use on cotton tripled from 1965 to 1967 In Texas, dose needed to kill bollworm increased many 1000-fold 1960–65 Plants resistant to insects Introducing natural enemies	Risky Self-defeating
Health	DDT combats malaria	Experience in Panama and other parts of world	DDT may affect sex-hormone metabolism	Birds and mammals have similar sex hormones and regulators High DDT levels in autopsies of humans	Probably dangerous

Source: Jerrold R. Coombs and Milton Meux, "Teaching Strategies for Value Analysis," in Lawrence Metcalf, ed., Values Education: Rationale, Strategies, and Procedures (Washington, D.C.: National Council for the Social Studies, 1971), p. 43.

toward factual assertions. Factual statements should be appraised in light of such questions as

1. How do you know this is true?
2. What evidence is there to indicate that this is true?
3. Who said this is the case?
4. Why should we believe what this person says?
5. Do other authorities agree with what he says? [8]

4. Clarifying the relevance of facts. Students must judge the relevance of facts in terms of the general point of view and the specific criteria on which the value decision is to be made. Students commonly err by considering facts that have no bearing on the viewpoint at hand. In attempting to decide whether a judge is morally fit to sit on the U.S. Supreme Court, for example, a student may consider the number of trials over which the judge presided that were reversed for procedural mistakes. Although this fact might have valence in assessing the overall competence of a judge, it is not necessarily relevant to a decision about his moral competence.

In like manner, a student may keep the point of view firmly in mind, but harness a fact on the basis of a dubious criterion. For example, a student might argue that welfare is morally wrong because it gives money to people who haven't earned it. Here the student's criterion is that receiving unearned money is a moral wrong. Yet, when questioned, the student concedes that there is nothing morally wrong about people inheriting money they haven't worked for. That welfare recipients receive unearned money thus becomes irrelevant because the criterion that sustained it is rejected.

The evidence card is a concrete device that helps determine the relevance of facts. A sample evidence card might contain the following information: [9]

Value
judgment: Welfare is morally wrong. (Moral point of view)

Fact: Welfare gives money to people
           who haven't earned it.

Criterion: Practices that give money to
people who haven't earned it
are morally wrong. (Moral point of view)

On the back of the card, supporting evidence and contrary evidence can be included, as can reasons for believing or rejecting the criterion.

5. *Arriving at a tentative value decision.* This is the culmination of the preceding four tasks. It is simply a decision made in the light of the analysis up to that time.

6. *Testing the value principle implied in the decision.* A value decision is rational only if the evaluator can accept the value principle implied in the decision. Four tests to determine the adequacy of a value principle are available.

NEW CASES TEST

The value principle is explicitly formulated. Then the evaluator considers whether he or she can accept the judgments that follow by attempting to apply them to other relevant cases.

Teachers need to help students uncover the value principles embedded in their judgments, recognize analogous situations, and determine whether the principles hold equally well in these situations. For example:

S: I don't think we ought to have a guaranteed annual income, because some people would be getting money without working for it. (*S makes an evaluation and gives a reason to support it.*)

T: Do you think, then, that people ought not to get money without working for it? (*T formulates principle he thinks is implicit in S's evaluation.*)

S: Yes. (*S affirms principle formulated by T.*)

T: Some people inherit large amounts of money. They don't work for this money. Do you think they ought not to get it? (*T identifies new case and asks student if he can ac-*

cept the evaluation resulting from the application of the principle to this case.) [10]

SUBSUMPTION TEST

The value principle is explicitly formulated. Then the evaluator attempts to assemble facts which show that the value principle is an instance of some more general value principle that he or she accepts. For example:

T: You think, then, that any commercial venture that is hazardous to sea life is undesirable. (*T formulates principle implicit in S's evaluation.*)

S: Yes. (*S affirms principle formulated by T.*)

T: Why? (*T probes for more general principle.*)

S: Because it is a bad thing to endanger resources needed for sustaining human life. (*S gives more general value principle.*)

T: What has that to do with regarding commercial ventures which are dangerous to sea life as undesirable? (*T tries to elicit facts to complete the subsuming argument.*)

S: Sea life produces food and much of the oxygen that is needed to support human life.[11]

ROLE EXCHANGE TEST

The evaluator imaginatively exchanges roles with someone else affected by the application of the principle. Then the evaluator considers whether he or she can still accept the principle as it applies in this role. For example:

S: I think everyone who goes to college should be exempted from the draft.

T: Suppose you couldn't go to college because you didn't have enough money or good enough grades. Would you still feel that everyone who goes to college should be exempted from the draft? [12]

UNIVERSAL CONSEQUENCES TEST

The evaluator imagines what the consequences would be if everyone in similar circumstances were to engage in the action being evaluated. Then the evaluator considers whether to accept these consequences. For example:

S: I don't see anything wrong with refusing to pay my income tax when the government is going to use it for something I don't approve of.

T: Have you considered what would happen to the government and the country if people refused to pay income tax when they thought the government was going to use it for something they didn't approve of? [13]

In inviting students to test the adequacy of their value principles, the teacher encourages more complex, more comprehensive, and more consistent reasoning. The value analysis tests are similar to the "probes" developed in Kohlberg's model. Moreover, Coombs is aware that these tests must be adapted to the developmental stage of the students. Individuals at lower stages of ego development have a tendency to polarize problems, to seek closure abruptly, to blur the distinction between means and ends, and to be easily swayed by sources of high status or power. In an unmediated form, the value analysis tests might appear more as an assault than an aid to these students. The teacher must respect the students' capacity to tolerate ambiguity and complexity.

Coombs does not specify in any systematic way how the teacher can accommodate the various stages of ego development, although he alludes to Kohlberg's work as a possible guide. But, except for a couple of general suggestions, the reader must fashion a developmentally sensitive pedagogy.

Conflict Resolution Tasks

Value conflict resolution is an important sequel to value analysis in the Coombs model. No other model of values education focuses so explicitly on this area. The foundation of the

Coombs-Meux version of conflict resolution is the premise that causes of value conflict, and the "psychological meaning" of conflict to the parties involved are not directly relevant for the resolution process and can be ignored.[14] The assumption is that if value judgments conflict, the source of the conflict must be a difference in the way one or more of the six tasks of value analysis were carried out. The implication is that if people all followed the same analytic procedure, differences in value judgments would be minimized.

The six tasks of conflict resolution directly parallel the steps of value analysis. Essentially, conflicts are to be resolved by reducing differences in students' treatment of the value analysis techniques.

1. Reducing differences in the interpretation of the value question. This procedure is self-evident. When students assume different points of view or assign different meanings to value objects, the teacher must help them find common ground or realize that, failing common ground, their evaluations may conflict.

2. Reducing differences in the purported facts assembled. If conflict stems from a confusion of factual and evaluative statements, the teacher must clarify the distinction between these two kinds of assertions. If students have varying quality and quantity of evidence as a result of using different sources, the teacher can encourage the sharing of data.

3. Reducing differences in the assessed truth of purported facts. Differences in the assessed truth of facts may stem from problems in scientific method or rules of evidence—a student may confuse correlation with causation, for example. Or, students may use different standards of strictness concerning evidence. They may disagree on how many facts are needed to support a generalization. The teacher needs to bring these sources of tension to the surface and invite students to examine them critically, with an eye toward reaching consensus.

4. Reducing differences in the relevance of facts. Generally, relevance differences hinge on the different weight attached to value criteria. For example, to a person who cares a great deal about health but little about economics, the fact that air pollution may cause emphysema is of primary importance. A more economically minded individual may single out for paramount consideration the fact that attempts to curb air pollution through installing expensive controls would raise the price of automobiles.

The teacher can ask students to clarify differences in criteria emphasis and explore the implications of such differences: "John and Bill, what implications do you think your differences might have? Bill, since you consider that fact about DDT to be irrelevant, what would that imply for you with respect to actions you might take or recommend, plans you might adopt or recommend, and so forth?" [15]

Typically, when light is cast on differences in criteria, these differences are reduced. Students may unknowingly be giving more priority to a specific concern than they would if they were to reflect on the matter explicitly.

5. *Reducing differences in tentative value decisions.* These differences often arise when students come to a tentative value judgment prematurely or formulate it in overly general terms. As a remedy, the teacher might propose that a general value judgment be split into two or more specific value judgments: "John and Bill, although you disagree about whether DDT is good [a general value term], you may agree that DDT is cheap and practical [both specific value terms], but still disagree on whether DDT is safe [a specific value term]." [16]

6. *Reducing differences in testing the acceptability of value principles.* Differences in the acceptability of value principles are "reduced by increasing the base of consideration and experience common to the evaluators in the tests of their principles." [17] In essence, students are asked to consider common new cases, common new roles, and common new consequences.

In a model conflict resolution session in *Values Education*, a role-exchange test is used to explore differences in value principles and suggest points of agreement. The issue under discussion is a proposed guaranteed minimum yearly income (GMYI). Two students, Keith and Terry, state their value principles as follows:

K: Any GMYI that brings 34.1 million people to nonpoverty status without nullifying the gain is desirable even though it may result in work disincentive and a rise in prices for nonpoverty levels of income, and even though it probably will have much opposition in Congress.

T: Any GMYI that increases the federal budget from $4 billion to $7 billion over the present proposed budget, adds more people to tax-supported programs, and duplicates benefits is undesirable, even though it sets national standards for welfare payments and brings a significant number of lower-level income families to nonpoverty level.[18]

During the role-exchange test, in which Keith is asked to assume the perspective of a middle-income taxpayer and Terry is requested to act-out an indigent person dependent on the GMYI, Terry, in particular, is moved to view the issue in a new light. His value principle concerning the GMYI is not explicitly or formally changed as a result of the role-exchange experience, but it is held with more compassion:

T: When the role exchange was with the person who would have received benefits had the plan been instituted, I didn't change my value principle but did empathize with those people. The realization that I might not have enough money to sustain me heightened my moral concern and played down the economic concern. My feelings that prompted this change in concerns included despair, hostility toward everybody that had more, and anxiety about family well-being.[19]

The teacher asks Terry how he regards his original value principle. He replies:

T: I feel like it stands, pretty much the way it is. However, the more I talk about it, the more the moral concern has than the economic, because it'll come out every time we talk about the economy because Keith will bring it up.[20]

The upshot of this dialogue is that Terry continues to hold to his position, but with a greater sense of tentativeness and qualification (which recalls James Shaver's discussion of "qualified decision making" in the rationale building model). Keith, too, reaffirms his commitment to the GMYI, but takes the threat of inflation more seriously. Both Keith and Terry recognize the differences between them but become more aware of their common concerns.

Coombs and Meux are careful to point out that failure to achieve a complete resolution of a value conflict is not necessarily a sign of faulty pedagogy. Perhaps factors in the value situation (e.g., giving different weight to different criteria) that produced the conflicting value judgments in the first place still operate at the conclusion of the deliberative process. Nonetheless, even when total resolution is not achieved, the conflict resolution process is not without effect. One of the more important outcomes is that a significant reduction in conflict may take place *within* each person. Any controversial question that is significant to an individual will engage two or more conflicting values. In the case of Terry (in the GMYI issue), the conflict was between his economic and moral concerns; the articulation of criteria and the testing of principles brought the relative importance of these two concerns into sharper focus. Conflict resolution procedures may thus reduce *intra*personal, if not *inter*personal, conflict.[21]

In addition, the effort to resolve conflict may result in an increased understanding of others' perspectives. Terry's response suggests this benefit:

T: Do you know what I think this conflict resolution comes from? You take a main issue (it's pretty hard to resolve a main issue), but you get down into the smaller things and you start agreeing about those, and you build a little rap-

port there—getting to know how the other person feels.
. . . and that's a whole lot of it.[22]

Conflict resolution tasks, then, invite students to take others' perspectives, as well as their own new perspectives reflected in similar cases and hypothetical roles. In this respect it is consistent with Kohlberg's orientation, although Coombs seems to assume a more fluid progression of social-perspective-taking ability than Kohlberg and perhaps underplays the difficulties young children might experience in critical inquiry and principle testing. Clearly, however, the conflict resolution strategy is a worthy addition to the moral educator's repertoire of methods. Coombs' model is the only one to include such a strategy. It would seem to be effective in developing students' group-decision-making skills and promoting more adequate moral reasoning.

SUMMARY AND APPRAISAL

The basic strength of value analysis is that it provides a detailed, step-by-step process for analyzing value questions, particularly those complex public policy issues that involve a large number of facts and possible consequences. By engaging in the six procedures, the individual comes to a judgment based on strict standards of rationality. No other model presents such a thorough description of procedures for dealing with value issues.

Yet the strength of the approach may also be a weakness. Students could see value analysis as an academic exercise. Conceivably, students could work through the analytic procedures in class and continue to act in irrational ways outside class. Other projects in values education have identified this problem. Students could, as Newmann has noted, regard the highly systematized value analysis process as a "game" that has but marginal relevance to their real concerns. When they confront dilemmas and value questions in their daily lives, they have no time to build fact charts and evidence cards. Presumably, a transfer of value analysis to day-to-day questions could be made, but Coombs fails to treat this issue.

A second limitation is the lack of an affective component. Coombs refers to the findings of ego psychologists explicitly concerned with affect, but his discussion of ego development is restricted to conceptual or cognitive concerns. He ignores such ego-related functions as empathy, genuineness, and identity realization. There is little attention to the problem of engaging students' feelings about value situations, of how fantasies and imagination may be mobilized in value analysis. The approach is severely logical. Used exclusively, many issues might be "intellectualized" to the point of alienating students. Ideally, the Coombs model would be supplemented by other approaches, such as the consideration model and values clarification, to accommodate affective concerns.

REFERENCES

Principal Sources

Evans, W. K.; T. P. Applegate; G. G. Casper; and R. W. Tucker. *Rational Value Decisions and Value Conflict Resolution: A Handbook for Teachers.* Salt Lake City, Utah: ESEA Title III Office, n.d.
This is a handbook to help the teacher implement the Metcalf value analysis program. Actual lessons are presented for use in the classroom.

Fraenkel, Jack. *How to Teach About Values: An Analytic Approach.* Englewood Cliffs, N.J.: Prentice-Hall, 1977.
Fraenkel presents values analysis as an approach to values education along with values clarification and Kohlberg's theory.

Metcalf, Lawrence, ed. *Values Education: Rationale, Strategies, and Procedures.* Washington, D.C.: National Council for the Social Studies, 1971.
This book includes four essays that outline the objectives and procedures involved in value analysis. This is a thorough presentation of the approach; classroom procedures are outlined in detail.

Meux, Milton, et al. *Value Analysis Capability Development Programs: Final Report.* Salt Lake City, Utah: Granite School District and the Value Analysis Capability Development Programs University of Utah, 1974.
This book presents curriculum materials to help students develop competence in rational value analysis.

Related Readings

Durkin, Mary C., and Anthony H. Durkin. *McNaughton Taba Program in Social Science.* Menlo Park, Calif.: Addison Wesley, 1974.

This is a program for the elementary level designed to develop analytic skills in relation to value related issues.

Fraenkel, Jack R., series ed. *Perspective in World Order.* New York: Random House, 1973, 1975.

These are curriculum materials for grades 8–12 that employ the value analysis approach. Booklets deal with peacekeeping and human rights, as well as other issues.

7
THE COGNITIVE MORAL DEVELOPMENT MODEL

The previous chapters have centered on a variety of dimensions in the construction of moral education models: moral education in the context of democracy, as increasing one's ability to clarify values issues, as consideration for others, and with the use of data and logical inquiry. Lawrence Kohlberg's cognitive moral development model attends to each of these concerns and introduces a new emphasis—the development of moral reasoning. Kohlberg has combined work in philosophy, psychology, and educational practice to construct a comprehensive explanation of moral development and a model for moral education.

Kohlberg's approach to moral education rests on a clear distinction between moral and nonmoral values and a precise formulation of the role of conflict in moral decision making. Kohlberg's theory of moral development and moral education considers moral judgment as representing a naturally autonomous thought process. Moral thinking must be understood on its own terms, Kohlberg argues, and not simply as an expression of a general valuing process. Moreover, moral judgment necessarily involves choosing among competing values. Awareness of moral values is just one step toward the more critical responsibility of weighing these values against one another as they conflict in concrete situations of choice.

Although we refer to Kohlberg's theory as a theory of moral development, more precisely it is a theory of the development of moral *judgment*. Traditionally, morality has been equated with "good" character, or with "proper" behavior. For Kohlberg, morality is most powerfully explained in terms of the logical processes through which one conceives and resolves moral conflicts. Morality hinges on the form in which moral choices are justified. A student may affirm the values of honesty and loyalty, for example. But she exercises her capacity for moral judgment only when a problematic situation forces her to set these values against each other and assign priorities to them. Such a situation may arise if the student discovers that her friend has cheated on a test. The notions of honesty and loyalty send cross-messages. Should she tell the teacher about the wrongdoing, or keep her friend's confidence? What reveals the quality of an individual's moral judgment is not the choice per se, but the pattern of reasoning with which he or she justifies the choice.

What distinguishes Kohlberg's approach from other models that emphasize reason in moral valuing is his theory of the stages of moral judgment. Kohlberg does not simply say that children should learn to choose values, or to mediate value conflicts, on the basis of reason. He has delineated empirically the structure of moral reasoning and its transformations from middle childhood to adulthood. A seven-year-old's definition of moral reasonableness, Kohlberg has shown, is fundamentally different from that of a seventeen-year-old. The moral educator must be careful to keep these developmental differences in mind.

At the heart of Kohlberg's theory is the concept of "stages." Stages refer to the structure of reasoning and imply the following characteristics:

1. Stages are "structured wholes," organized systems of thought. This means that individuals are consistent in their level of moral judgment.
2. Stages form an invariant sequence. Under all conditions except trauma, movement is always forward, never backward.

Individuals never skip stages, and movement is always to the next stage. This is true in all cultures.

3. Stages are "hierarchical integrations." Thinking at a higher stage includes or comprehends within it lower-stage thinking. There is a tendency to function at or prefer the highest available stage.

It is important to note that a later stage is "higher" than an earlier one because it can more adequately organize the multiplicity of facts, interests, and possibilities life holds in store. As we shall see, Kohlberg's position is that higher stages of moral judgment are superior to lower stages not only in a philosophic sense but also because they are more socially adaptive.

One further note about the concept of stages. Children do not develop cognitive stages the way they learn specific skills, knowledge, and attitudes. Even though stages depend on experience for their formation, they are not direct reflections of the child's culture and external world. Mental structures are not merely products of society; they develop as a result of the interaction between the child and the world. This interaction leads to a restructuring of the child's cognitive organization rather than to the direct imposition of the culture's pattern on the child.[1] In other words, a child does not receive society's values (e.g., a respect for property or the importance of truth) as if his or her mind were an empty container. The child accepts, or assimilates, these values in accordance with a personal, internal logic. The child does not simply mirror the culture's moral images but interprets them in a way that is qualitatively different from an adult's interpretation. At the same time, in confronting social reality and trying to make sense of it, the child's structure of thinking changes. As the child begins to play games with peers, for example, he or she gradually constructs a concept of fair exchange. Interactions with others lead the child to develop the perspective of rules as being necessary. The culture does not impose this perspective; the child develops it, in a sense, naturally to accommodate to increasingly complex social experiences. Stages thus shape, and are in turn shaped by, social experience. The teacher's task is complex, for he or she must appreciate students' current stage of judgment while creating an environment that will promote stage advancement.

A stage of moral judgment is reflected in the overall pattern of an individual's responses to moral dilemmas. Neither researchers nor teachers can determine a person's stage of moral thinking on the basis of answers to a single dilemma. It is only in the interests of economy and clarity, as we explain the six stages of moral judgment in this chapter, that we concentrate on only one dilemma to show how typical responses to it express each stage. The sample dilemma, commonly referred to as the Heinz dilemma, has been used with both children and adults. It follows below. The accompanying questions are designed to probe the logic of the respondent's solution.

In Europe, a woman was near death from a special kind of cancer. There was one drug that the doctors thought might save her. It was a form of radium that a druggist in the same town had recently discovered. The drug was expensive to make, but the druggist was charging ten times what the drug cost him to make. He paid $200 for the radium and charged $2,000 for a small dose of the drug. The sick woman's husband, Heinz, went to everyone he knew to borrow the money, but he could only get together about $1,000, which is half of what it cost. He told the druggist that his wife was dying, and asked him to sell the drug cheaper or let him pay later. But the druggist said, "No, I discovered the drug and I'm going to make money from it." So Heinz gets desperate and considers breaking into the man's store to steal the drug for his wife.

1. Should Heinz steal the drug? Why or why not?
2. If Heinz doesn't love his wife, should he steal the drug for her? Why or why not?
3. Suppose the person who is dying is not his wife but a stranger. Should Heinz steal the drug for a stranger? Why or why not?
4. (If you favor stealing the drug for a friend:) Suppose it's a pet animal he loves. Should Heinz steal to save the pet animal? Why or why not?

5. Why should people do everything they can to save another's life, anyhow?
6. It is against the law for Heinz to steal. Does that make it morally wrong? Why or why not?
7. Why should people generally do everything they can to avoid breaking the law, anyhow?
7a. How does this relate to Heinz's case?

DEFINITION OF STAGES

In Kohlberg's framework, moral development in all cultures follows a three-level progression from an egocentric through a societal to a universal perspective (see table 7.1). An individual's moral judgment grows less and less dependent on immediate personal and interpersonal reference points and, in the highest stages, becomes anchored in universal principles of justice. The highest stages are most able to handle moral complexity in a stable and consistent way.

The Preconventional Level

At the preconventional level, an individual approaches a moral issue from the perspective of his or her concrete interests. A child at this level is not concerned with what society defines as the right way to behave in a certain situation, but only with the concrete consequences (punishment, reward, exchange of favors) of action. This perspective focuses on the child's pursuing concrete interests while avoiding untenable risks.

Stage 1: The punishment-and-obedience orientation. The child who reasons at this stage thinks only in terms of physical problems and physical solutions. What is right is what avoids punishment. A typical stage 1 response to the Heinz dilemma is that Heinz *cannot* disobey the authorities, for he will be severely punished if he does. The child believes that Heinz is unable to defy authority; the punishment that would follow would be too great to bear.

Stage 2: The instrumental-relativist orientation. During stage 2 a new standard of judgment arises: the standard of *fairness*. It is

TABLE 7.1. THE SIX STAGES OF MORAL JUDGMENT

	Content of Stage		
Level and Stage	What Is Right	Reasons for Doing Right	Social Perspective of Stage
Level I: Preconventional Stage 1: Heteronomous morality	To avoid breaking rules backed by punishment, obedience for its own sake, and avoiding physical damage to persons and property.	Avoidance of punishment, and the superior power of authorities.	*Egocentric point of view.* Doesn't consider the interests of others or recognize that they differ from the actor's; doesn't relate two points of view. Actions are considered physically rather than in terms of psychological interests of others. Confusion of authority's perspective with one's own.
Stage 2: Individualism, instrumental purpose, and exchange	Following rules only when it is to someone's immediate interest; acting to meet one's own interests and needs and letting others do the same. Right is also what's fair—what's an equal exchange, a deal, an agreement.	To serve one's own needs or interests in a world where you have to recognize that other people have their interests, too.	*Concrete individualistic perspective.* Aware that everybody has his or her own interests to pursue and these conflict, so that right is relative (in the concrete individualistic sense).
Level II: Conventional Stage 3: Mutual interpersonal expectations, relationships, and interpersonal conformity	Living up to what is expected by people close to you or what people generally expect of people in your role as son, brother, friend, etc. "Being	The need to be a good person in your own eyes and those of others. Your caring for others. Belief in the Golden Rule. Desire to maintain rules and au-	*Perspective of the individual in relationships with other individuals.* Aware of shared feelings, agreements, and expectations which take primacy

	"good" is important and means having good motives, showing concern about others. It also means keeping mutual relationships, such as trust, loyalty, respect.	thority that support stereotypical good behavior.	over individual interests. Relates points of view through the concrete Golden Rule, putting yourself in the other guy's shoes. Does not yet consider generalized system perspective.
Stage 4: Social system and conscience	Fulfilling the actual duties to which you have agreed. Laws are to be upheld except in extreme cases where they conflict with other fixed social duties. Right is also contributing to society, the group, or institution.	To keep the institution going as a whole, to avoid the breakdown in the system "if everyone did it," or the imperative of conscience to meet one's defined obligations. (Easily confused with stage 3 belief in rules and authority.)	*Differentiates societal point of view from interpersonal agreement or motives.* Takes the point of view of the system that defines roles and rules. Considers individual relations in terms of place in the system.
Level III: Postconventional, or Principled Stage 5: Social contract, or utility, and individual rights	Being aware that people hold a variety of values and opinions, that most values and rules are relative to your group. These relative rules should usually be upheld, in the interest of impartiality and because they are the social contract. Some nonrelative values and rights like *life* and *liberty*, however, must be upheld in any society and regardless of majority opinion.	A sense of obligation to law because of one's social contract to make and abide by laws for the welfare of all and for the protection of all people's rights. A feeling of contractual commitment, freely entered upon, to family, friendship, trust, and work obligations. Concern that laws and duties be based on rational calculation of overall utility, "the greatest good for the greatest number."	*Prior-to-society perspective.* Perspective of a rational individual aware of values and rights prior to social attachments and contracts. Integrates perspectives by formal mechanisms of agreement, contract, objective impartiality, and due process. Considers moral and legal points of view; recognizes that they sometimes conflict and finds it difficult to integrate them.

TABLE 7.1.—Continued

Level and Stage	Content of Stage		Social Perspective of Stage
	What Is Right	Reasons for Doing Right	
Level III: Postconventional, or Principled (continued) Stage 6: Universal ethical principles	Following self-chosen ethical principles. Particular laws or social agreements are usually valid because they rest on such principles. When laws violate these principles, one acts in accordance with the principle. Principles are universal principles of justice: the equality of human rights and respect for the dignity of human beings as individual persons.	The belief as a rational person in the validity of universal moral principles, and a sense of personal commitment to them.	*Perspective of a moral point of view from which social arrangements derive.* Perspective is that of any rational individual recognizing the nature of morality or the fact that persons are ends in themselves and must be treated as such.

Source: Lawrence Kohlberg, "Moral Stages and Moralization: The Cognitive-Developmental Approach," in *Moral Development and Behavior: Theory, Research, and Social Issues,* ed. Thomas Lickona (New York: Holt, Rinehart and Winston, 1976), pp. 34–35.

only fair that someone who has a good reason for doing something be judged by that reason and not by the arbitrary will of an authority figure. Authority, the central value of stage 1, is relativized at stage 2. An authority becomes like everybody else insofar as he or she has to play by the rules of the game, which are the rules of fairness.

The stage 2 rules of fairness, however, are interpreted in a physical, pragmatic way. Reciprocity is a matter of "you scratch my back and I'll scratch yours" and does not involve loyalty, gratitude, or justice. Fairness is certainly a moral category, but at stage 2 fairness means that everyone has a right to get away with what he or she can. From this preconventional perspective, if a teacher gives a test and does not proctor it carefully, it is fair for students to cheat. "Who is it hurting," a student at this stage will ask, "if I take my answers from his sheet?" The answer that it is hurting oneself does not yet make sense. How is it hurting oneself if the student gains points and nobody loses anything? Harm is understood only as a concrete reference; a vague sense of hurting oneself simply does not register. No wonder teachers have so much trouble convincing students that cheating is morally wrong.

In terms of Heinz and the druggist, most stage 2 subjects have no trouble in seeing how the druggist is causing Heinz great harm. They see it as natural for Heinz to want to steal the drug, given, that is, that he cares about his wife. If he does not—which is his business—then he probably would not take the risk. Why bother? Stage 2 respondents do not see a husband as having an obligation to his wife. Rather, husbands have the right to steal for their wives *if they want to*. Moreover, if Heinz does steal, it is most likely, in their opinion, that he will not be punished. What judge would not understand why Heinz stole? What better reason to steal than to save a wife's life? At a preconventional level, the issue of law does not arise except insofar as something to be "gotten around" in order to fulfill one's legitimate needs. In the Heinz dilemma the action takes place entirely from the perspective of the individuals involved: Heinz, his wife, the druggist, and the judge.

In our society, stage 2 begins to develop around the age of

seven or eight and remains the dominant stage throughout the grade school years. Studies of adolescents show that among the middle-class population, stage 2 reasoning recedes considerably, but it remains fairly dominant among working- and lower-class youth. Among adults it continues to persist, but more as a minor stage.

The Conventional Level

At the conventional level a person approaches a moral problem from a member-of-society perspective. The individual realizes and takes into consideration that the group or society expects actions to be in accordance with its moral norms. One strives not only to avoid punishment or censure but also to live up to the accepted definitions of a good person or role-occupant.

Stage 3: The interpersonal concordance or "good boy–nice girl" orientation. At stage 3, the motivation for moral action becomes fulfilling the expectations of significant others. As the reasons for doing right change, so does the concept of what is right in relation to others. Stage 2 reasoners think it right to simply pursue their own interests without unduly harming anybody else. At Stage 3, more is expected of self and others. The awareness that others have positive expectations of you leads to a new view of interpersonal relations. When two people enter a relationship, they place their trust in each other and expect that the other will be caring and respect that trust. A relationship is more than an equal exchange of benefits (as it is viewed at stage 2); it involves mutual commitment. To break that commitment or violate trust becomes for a stage 3 person what acting unfairly is for a stage 2 person: the cardinal wrongdoing.

The Heinz dilemma amply demonstrates this point. What are Heinz's obligations to his wife? From a stage 2 perspective, Heinz does not have any obligations per se. He certainly has the right to steal to save his wife's life if he wants to; but if he does not want to do this, neither his wife nor anyone else has any legitimate gripe against him. From a stage 3 perspective, by being married to this woman, Heinz has definite commitments to her. He should care for her and try to save her life. (Whether this includes stealing for her, however, is a point on which stage 3 respondents do not agree.) Even if he no longer loves his wife, the fact that he once loved her and committed himself to her means that he should be concerned about her.

In relation to the druggist, stage 2 respondents believe him to be basically within his rights to pursue profit; although he may be foolish not to give Heinz a break (and hence incur his retaliation), he has no obligation to do so. Stage 3 respondents, in contrast, often get angry just thinking about the druggist: "What kind of man is he? Doesn't he have a heart? He may not have known Heinz personally, but as a druggist and a member of the medical profession, he committed himself to help cure people, and now he is turning Heinz away for purely selfish reasons." Selfishness, from a stage 3 perspective, is another form of violating trust and commitment and is almost always wrong.

Stage 3 begins to develop among preadolescents; is the dominant stage during adolescence; and along with stage 4, remains the dominant stage for most adults in our society. It is a mature (or equilibrated) structure insofar as it proves an adequate mode for dealing with most conflicts that arise among people who know one another. Its inadequacy surfaces when an individual must deal with problems on a societal level. For such problems, stages 4 and above prove more adequate.

Stage 4: Social system and conscience. If stage 3 role taking is primarily characterized by the ability to take the third-person perspective of *significant* others, stage 4 role taking is primarily characterized by the ability to take the shared point of view of the *generalized* other. That is, a person takes the perspective of the social system in which he or she participates: the society and the various institutions with which one is affiliated.

The ability to view social problems from the perspective of the whole system usually provides a new basis for moral judgment. Let us turn again to the Heinz dilemma. Stage 3 respondents are primarily concerned with Heinz's commitments as a husband and with the druggist's inhumanity and failure to live up to what is expected of his profession; they are not usually concerned with how Heinz's decision affects the social system. From a stage 4 perspective, however, the effect on the social system becomes a major concern. People at this stage agree that Heinz is obligated to help save his wife and that the druggist has acted inhumanely, but they are also concerned that if Heinz were to steal, he would be weakening the moral order of society. *Law* emerges for them as a central value. They are not necessarily advocates of a "law and order" position; nevertheless, they appreciate that any society is bound together by social and moral agreements, many of which are codified into laws, and that any action which breaks those agreements threatens to a degree the solidarity and cohesion of the social system.

This is not to say that most stage 4 respondents decide that Heinz ought *not* to steal to save his wife. For even as they appreciate the centrality of law, so they appreciate the centrality of the value of life. In a sense, this dilemma is hardest to resolve at stage 4. Respondents realize that human life is sacred and that law's purpose is often to guard the sacredness of life. Thus, when the values of law and life openly conflict, they have trouble choosing between them.

Stage 4 reasoning begins to develop before mid-adolescence. It is a highly equilibrated stage and often proves to be the highest stage to which adults develop. It adequately handles societal as well as interpersonal issues. Still, Kohlberg believes that it is not adequate for dealing with situations in which a system of laws or beliefs comes into conflict with basic human rights. If a person lives in a society in which the legal system systematically denies to some people basic human rights, should that person agree that in order to preserve the social and moral order, he or she ought not to protest or even violate what are considered to be unjust laws? Stage 4 reasoning has no adequate response to this question. For while people at this stage may argue for working within the system for change, if the system itself is based on unjust discrimination, they are forced to choose between adherence and dissent. Kohlberg believes that within the structure of stage 4 reasoning, there are no criteria for choosing dissent over adherence. He has therefore delineated postconventional stages that can deal more adequately with these moral conflicts.

Postconventional, Autonomous, or Principled Level

At this level, an individual approaches a moral problem from a prior-to-society perspective. That is, the person can see beyond the given norms and laws of his or her society and ask, "What are the principles upon which any good society is based?"

Stages 5 and 6: Social contract and universal ethical principles. These are the stages of principled moral reasoning and are the most controversial stages in Kohlberg's theory. They are philosophically derived, but some moral philosophers disagree with Kohlberg's formulation of the "highest" stages. There is less empirical data on these than on the other stages, and they have therefore been questioned more seriously by psychologists.

Stage 5 defines right action in terms of general individual rights and standards that have been critically examined and agreed upon by the whole society. Moral obligation is seen from the perspective of a social contract. The advantage of this concept is that it does not attempt to prescribe a fixed formula of obligation for each relationship, as is usually done at stage 4. Rather, legal and social commitments are viewed as something to which each partner to the contract freely obligates himself or herself, knowing that the others have equally and freely obligated themselves. Their mutual agreements define the nature of their obligations to one another. Contracts, either in the form of public law or more personal contracts such as friendship or marriage, are not inherently good or bad unless they involve an abrogation of such basic human rights as life and liberty. Such contracts would be morally invalid. Thus, for example, even if one person voluntarily sells himself into slavery, the other does not have the moral right to hold him to that.

The following is a stage 5 response to the Heinz dilemma:

> What Heinz did was not wrong. The distribution of scarce drugs should be regulated by principles of fairness. In the absence of such

regulations, the druggist was within his legal rights, but in the circumstances he has no moral complaint. He still was within his moral rights, however, unless it was within his society a strongly disapproved thing to do. While what Heinz did was not wrong, it was not his duty to do it. In this case it is not wrong for Heinz to steal the drug, but it goes beyond the call of duty; it is a deed of supererogation.[2]

The respondent begins with what should ideally be agreed upon in any society: "The distribution of scarce drugs should be regulated by principles of fairness." But since this was not the agreed-upon principle in Heinz's society, the druggist "was within his moral rights." Heinz has no duty to steal, for that is not part of the usual contract between husband and wife. Yet, if he does steal, it would be a "deed of supererogation," a good deed beyond the call of duty.

Kohlberg's dissatisfaction with this response and with moral reasoning based on the concept of social contract has led him to formulate the "higher" stage 6. His thinking about this stage has been strongly influenced by the Harvard philosopher John Rawls.[3] Kohlberg cites the following response to the Heinz dilemma as an example of stage 6 reasoning.

If the husband does not feel very close or affectionate to his wife, should he steal the drug?
Yes. The value of her life is independent of any personal ties. The value of human life is based on the fact that it offers the only possible source of a categorical moral "ought" to a rational being acting in the role of a moral agent.
Suppose it were a friend or an acquaintance?
Yes, the value of a human life remains the same.[4]

The difference here is that the respondent does not make the act of stealing contingent upon any prior agreement between Heinz and the other person involved, but rather sees it as a categorical moral "ought" that any rational being acting the role of a moral agent would accept as his duty to perform. The ethical principles underlying stage 6 thinking transcend the agreements of a given social contract. They are the universal principles of justice, of the reciprocity and equality of human rights, and of respect for the dignity of human beings as individual persons.

Moral reasoning at the principled level is more adequate because it takes into account more points of view and is applied in a more consistent manner. A principled approach views moral conflict from the perspective of any human being, not merely members of a person's society or religion. From the perspective of one's own society, for example, it might make sense to say people ought to be loyal to their country. But would a conventional American also want dissidents in the Soviet Union to stop their protest and be loyal to their country? Apparently not, given the popular response in this country to Soviet dissidents. How, though, can one consistently maintain a rule of loyalty to one's country and yet encourage disloyalty in other countries? One can do so only by maintaining a principle of being primarily loyal to the preserving of human rights and secondarily loyal to one's country insofar as it preserves human rights. Then, consistent, universalizable criteria could apply to a person in any country who has to decide when to protest and when to support his or her country's actions.

By following a particular philosophic definition of morality, Kohlberg has been able to join philosophy to psychology. He has been able to delineate what a highest stage of moral judgment would have to be like in order to qualify by those philosophic criteria as "truly moral." Given that definition, he was able to trace the logical steps through which moral judgment develops from its point of emergence in childhood until it reaches that highest stage. But in achieving that degree of clarity, Kohlberg has had to accept two important limitations. The first is the criticism by other philosophers that his definition of the highest stages is too narrow. Perhaps there are more possible versions of principled morality than the ones Kohlberg delineates. The second is that he has limited moral development to the development of moral judgment. Moral judgment may be an essential ingredient of moral development, but it is not by any means the whole picture.

MORAL EDUCATION: AN OVERVIEW OF KOHLBERG'S EDUCATIONAL WORK

There have been two strands in Kohlberg's educational work. One has involved incorporating in the classroom curriculum a concern for the discussion of moral issues and the stimulation of moral growth. The other has involved restructuring the school environment to allow for greater democratic participation by the students in the school's governing process.

On the basis of his experience with discussion-oriented programs of moral education, Kohlberg has concluded that moral change is most likely to occur when the discussions succeed in arousing cognitive conflict among the participants. A participant who is exposed to views based on moral reasoning higher than his or her own may become unsure of the adequacy of the original position and begin to consider the merits of other positions. The participant does not then simply switch positions, but begins the process of restructuring his or her own way of reasoning about moral issues.

Although moral discussion programs have succeeded in stimulating moral growth, it is clear that by themselves they do not constitute a curriculum for moral education. They are generally not integrated into the larger curriculum nor do they aim to affect the students' educational experience in more than a limited way. Kohlberg has clearly stated that his goal is to develop a more encompassing program of moral education:

> If brief periods of classroom discussion can have a substantial effect on moral development, a pervasive, enduring and psychologically sound concern for the school's influence upon moral development should have much deeper effects. Such a concern would pervade the curriculum areas of social studies, law education, philosophy and sex education, rather than representing a new curriculum area. More deeply, it would affect the social atmosphere and justice structure of the school.[5]

In the years since 1970, Kohlberg, his colleagues, and his students have been working on extending the principles of developmental moral education to existing and beginning curriculums.

Parallel to this curriculum strand has been the effort to "affect the social atmosphere and justice structure of the school." Kohlberg believes that the "hidden curriculum" offers a rich opportunity for educators to involve students in moral learning. Although students can learn much from reading about and discussing social and moral issues, there is no substitute for participating in the deliberation on real-life social and moral issues. Because such issues arise naturally within the context of school life, why not, Kohlberg asks, use these opportunities for involving students in this deliberation? Why only teach about democracy when one can practice democracy within the context of the school?

Kohlberg has embarked on two experiments in educational democracy. The first was within the context of a prison; the second was with an alternative school within an urban high school. Both experimental programs are being evaluated for their effect on the moral development of their participants.

STRATEGIES OF MORAL EDUCATION [6]

The basis of moral education in the developmental model is that the teacher creates opportunities for students to think through their experiences in increasingly complex ways. What motivates students toward greater cognitive sophistication is exposure to more adequate patterns of reasoning, specifically those that reflect a stage of moral judgment one higher than their own. When individuals are forced to consider approaches to moral conflicts that are more comprehensive and consistent than those they are used to, cognitive "disequilibrium" results. The power of a more adequate logic is unsettling yet enticing. Over time, the encounter with higher-level thinking stimulates the self-development of a more advanced stage.

Cognitive disequilibrium results from the individual's ability to take the role of others. If people could not assume different points of view, they would see no conflict. As we have noted, an individual's capacity to adopt the perspective of others changes in quality with age. Elementary-age children need practice in walking in the shoes of a classmate or family member. Junior high students require help in focusing on the needs of the group. Students in high school may see conflicts from the legal or societal standpoint or, in some cases, from a more universal, principled vantage point. Teachers should help students feel at home with the social perspective and level of reasoning one stage higher than their own.

To help students develop more inclusive social perspectives and more objective lines of reasoning, the teacher must make effective use of moral dilemmas. Moral dilemmas may emerge from the examination of three kinds of data—hypothetical, content specific, and real or practical concerns. Hypothetical dilemmas like the Heinz dilemma are not based on facts, but they are believable. The major value in the use of hypothetical issues is that students have little personal involvement and thus are more willing to risk public discussion and generalize the principles involved. Content-based dilemmas are those based on data found in a particular discipline of study, such as President Truman's decision to drop the atom bomb, found in the study of American history. Content-based dilemmas have as an advantage the possibility of demonstrating to students the moral dimensions of the lives of people they are studying—that issues of morality transcend time and place. "Real" or practical dilemmas, such as "Should I tell the teacher that my friend is cheating on the test?" maximize emotional involvement and thus interest in the topic.

Whatever the source of the moral dilemma, helping students come to rational terms with it demands the teacher's skillful use of questioning strategies. Questioning, or probing, invites respondents to explore the logic of their assertions and to interact with classmates in a manner that challenges their general pattern of thought. Specifically, the "right" questions can stimulate cognitive conflict and social role taking.

There are at least two phases of questioning: initial and in-depth strategies. Initial strategies introduce teachers and students to the discussion of moral issues and continue to develop students' moral awareness. In-depth strategies focus on the elements of discussions which may lead to structural change in moral reasoning.

The teacher's role in the initial phase of discussion is (1) to ensure that students understand the moral dilemma or problem in question, (2) to help students confront the *moral* components inherent in the problem, (3) to elicit students' rationale for their judgments, and (4) to encourage students with different rationales to interact with one another.

The sequencing of qualitatively different questions and comments is important for the teacher to consider. This is necessary both because the teacher wants to stimulate moral development and because moral discussion involves risk taking. Peer pressure often discourages risk taking and can run counter to the goals of moral education if group norms discourage open and honest communication. A suggested series of different kinds of questions follows.

1. *Highlighting the moral issue.* These questions are usually dialogue starters that ask students to take a stand on a moral issue. They help students identify situations as dilemmas that require resolution of a conflict or choice. They usually imply a question of "should," "ought," or "right or wrong": Should Heinz steal the drug? Is it wrong to steal to save another person's life? Should people be punished for stealing under those circumstances? Such questions cast light on the particular elements in the situation that make the dilemma a moral one.

2. *Asking "why" questions.* These questions ask students to explain the reasons supporting their stand on a moral issue. Such questions give students the chance to see that they may hold the same position as other classmates, but for a very different reason. These differences in thinking patterns begin to stimulate interest and dialogue. Questions like Why do you think your solution to the dilemma is a good one? or What is the main reason you decided to resolve the problem as you did? are two common examples of "why" questions.

3. *Complicating the circumstances.* There are two kinds of probing questions or statements that complicate the original moral problem. The first adds new information or situations to

the original problem in order to increase the complexity and cognitive conflict inherent in the original situation. In the Heinz dilemma, for example, such questions might include the following: Suppose Heinz's wife had specifically told him to (or not to) steal the drug, would that make a difference in your position? Suppose the judge who was hearing Heinz's case were a friend of Heinz, should that make a difference in his decision? Such questions stimulate greater differentiation of thinking particularly in the area of role taking. A student is thereby urged to consider more than a single view of how to resolve the moral conflict.

A second kind of complicating question is asked in order to help students avoid "escape hatching" from the moral issue. Escape hatching usually occurs when students first discuss moral dilemmas. Often they feel uncomfortable taking the risk of facing squarely the question of what is right. They would rather escape from the moral problem entirely by changing the whole dilemma. Commonly they attempt to alter the facts of the dilemma, thereby effectively solving the problem by eliminating the conflict. For example, in a dilemma concerning the decision to throw certain people overboard from an overcrowded lifeboat drifting at sea, students often avoid confronting the dilemma by wanting to tie the extra people to the side of the boat with ropes. To help students face the moral question in this case, the teacher might say, "But for the moment, let's assume we can't tie them to the boat," or, "Suppose there were no ropes in the lifeboat." The teacher might also complicate the dilemma itself: "Suppose holding the ropes would sink the lifeboat—if you had to choose between a mother and her eighteen-year-old son, who would be cast overboard?"

It is important for teachers to respect the fact that some students feel uncomfortable with facing moral problems head-on and discussing them directly. The practice of reasoning through moral issues is usually new, and sometimes overwhelming, to students. The teacher's role is to facilitate the process of facing the moral issue, not to "push" students to do so. Over time, the peer group helps to assume the task of confronting the dilemma.

These three considerations—highlighting the moral issue, asking "why" questions, and complicating the circumstances—constitute the "core" of the introduction to moral discussion. They are designed to illuminate the breadth of reasoning about moral problems. The length of time that a teacher spends on these introductory efforts depends on the nature of the particular group of students and the teacher's developing ease in leading the discussions.

In-Depth Questioning Strategies

The second phase of a moral discussion format involves a focus in depth. The teacher's questioning techniques parallel this change. In-depth questions force students to grapple with competing claims and rival rationales. These are four general in-depth strategies: refining questions, highlighting contiguous-stage arguments, clarifying and summarizing, and role-taking techniques.

1. *Refining questions*. Questions should probe many sides of the same issue. A "should" or "why" question is not sufficient to stimulate stage change. Students need to hear extended arguments from one another so they can understand the reasoning and challenge each other's logic. Five kinds of in-depth probing questions have been identified by moral educators interested in effective questioning strategies.

A *clarifying probe* asks students to explain the terms they use, especially when the meaning of a statement is ambiguous or does not convey the reasoning behind the content. A clarifying probe is important so that teachers do not ascribe their meaning to students' words. An example might be as follows:

S: No, he shouldn't tell on his friend who cheated on the test. He might get in trouble.
T: What kind of trouble?
S: Well, his friend won't like him anymore. He might get back at him in some way. [*Elements of stage 2*]

An *issue-specific probe* is a question or statement that asks students to explore one moral issue related to the problem in question. "Issues" are different areas of focus in our moral judgment. A few such issues are authority, roles of affiliation and affection, contract obligations, and the value of life. By focusing on a particular issue in depth, students have the opportunity to explore fully the grounds of their beliefs. Examples:

Do you have any obligation to a stranger? What is the difference between one's responsibility to family or friends, and to a stranger?

Why do people have a responsibility to obey legal authority?

An *inter-issue probe* is one that seeks to stimulate the resolution of conflict between two moral issues. Often the priority of one issue over the other reflects the difference between two contiguous stages of moral reasoning, such as the value of friendship at stage 3 carrying greater weight than the value of protecting one's own interest, as conceptualized at stage 2. This kind of probe invites students to test the adequacy of their rationale for choosing one issue over the other. Examples:

Which is more important, loyalty to a friend, or obeying a law?

If it becomes necessary to steal in order to save someone's life, could you justify that decision? How?

A *role-switch probe* asks the student to assume the perspective of a different person in the conflict than the one the student is taking. This kind of probe is important for stimulating students' role-taking ability, since it gives them practice in trying to see the same situation through another person's eyes.

Example. *Using the situation whether to tell on a friend who was cheating on a test.*

Would the friend think you were wrong to tell in this situation? Be the teacher for a minute. What would she say you ought to do in this situation and why? What would your parents say you ought to do? What would your friend's parents say is the right thing to do?

A *universal-consequences probe* asks students to consider what would happen if they applied their reasoning so that everyone would follow it. This probe encourages students to try to come up with a moral decision that would reflect fairness equally to people in general. Such a probe tests the limits of the logical adequacy of the students' judgment. Examples:

What would happen if everyone decided to steal from other people in order to save the life of someone they knew?

What would happen if everyone in society started to disobey the law?

How could teachers run classrooms and help children learn if everyone cheated on tests?

2. *Highlighting contiguous-stage arguments.* A second in-depth questioning strategy involves the teacher's responsibility for highlighting arguments at contiguous stages of moral reasoning. It is the next higher stage of moral reasoning that stimulates a person's moral growth. Students at a higher stage will not "lose" that reasoning ability by interacting with people who reason at lower stages. However, they too need the stimulation of a reasoning pattern more complex than their own.

There are two opportunities to highlight contiguous-stage arguments. The first is when students themselves use contiguous stages in dialogue. Once teachers are able to "hear" the differences in reasoning patterns, they can begin to encourage students to explore the adequacy of their thinking: "Wendy, I noticed your reason was different from Peter's. Could you tell us again why you think your solution was a good one? How is it different from what Peter just said?"

A second occasion for highlighting contiguous-stage arguments occurs when the class is missing the perspective of a higher-stage argument. The teacher can then encourage students whose thinking often reflects elements of a higher stage to share that perspective on a new issue: "Carlo, you gave us an interesting solution to the problem we discussed yesterday when you talked about what's good for society. Could you or someone else tell us how that same argument might apply to the case we are discussing today?" Sometimes the whole group is unable to see a given moral conflict from more than one perspective, and no one offers a more adequate point of view. Then it is up to the *teacher* to pose arguments at the next higher stage: "I notice no one has mentioned what the law argues as the right thing to do in this case. The law says _____ based on the reasoning that _____. Could we hear some opinions about this legal point of view?"

3. Clarifying and summarizing. Another in-depth teaching strategy involves a shift in the teacher's role from initiating questions to clarifying and summarizing what students say. By this phase of discussion, students have learned how to approach questions of moral conflict; *they* can ask the open-ended questions. The teacher becomes a more active listener, linking crucial elements of discussion.

The teacher needs to monitor the discussion so that students become aware of the alternate reasoning patterns presented by their classmates. Although students learn to take more initiative in stimulating one another's thinking, the teacher still needs to maintain a focus that facilitates the developmental processes of cognitive conflict and role taking.

The following dialogue from an eleventh- and twelfth-grade psychology class demonstrates this shift in teacher role. The students have been discussing suicide and euthanasia at length. They take responsibility for addressing their comments to one another and elaborating and stimulating one another's thinking. The teacher can therefore direct attention to the group as a whole:

[Refocuses; highlights a new moral issue]

Teacher: The issue of suicide is important but maybe for the moment we should stick to the issue of euthanasia and whether or not it's right to take someone's life or at what point could it be right.

Mike: I don't think it could be right for a doctor to because a doctor doesn't know. . . . I'm again going back to the mind thing, right? A doctor doesn't know the mind of a person as well as someone close to them. Like you come up with all these questions like how do you know he's really gone in the mind? Well, a person's brother would know if he's gone in the mind and someone's brother could make the right decision I think. If you really love that person you'll do what you think. . . . If the right thing to do is kill that person that's what you'll do. [*Elements of stage 3*]

Jim: I wouldn't want to be the guy to tell them to do it.

Mike: I'm saying in a real extreme case . . . like say he just lost his girlfriend. I wouldn't say you know all right I'll kill you. He's suffering. His mind's gone. People feed him with needles. He never does anything by himself. If he asks me . . .

[Clarifies Mike's statement]

Karen: Oh, but if he didn't ask you you wouldn't take it on yourself.

Mike: No.

[Takes the perspective of others]	*Bob:*	That's such a personal evaluation. To you that's so much worse than losing a girlfriend like you said but for some people it might not be.
	Mike:	I'm saying if there's absolutely no hope whatsoever.
[Stimulates perspective taking]	*Karen:*	Who's to judge?
	Mike:	Someone who knows him extremely well is to judge.
[Complicates the circumstances]	*John:*	What if they don't have anyone who knows them very well?
	Lisa:	I think if the person themselves say they want to die.
[Highlights the moral issue]	*Jim:*	Just because you say you want to die does that give you the right to die?
	Lisa:	Yeah.
	Jim:	You could be wanting to die one time and another time you could be feeling a lot better. You could think to yourself, "Oh, I need to end it all now." You can think about it but I don't think a person has the right to decide "I should kill myself" when there's still a way or a reason to live.
[Asks a "why" question of himself]	*Mike:*	I'm saying when there's *absolutely* no hope. You look at them and sort of brush them aside. We've got to keep them alive because that's the thing you have to do. You have to keep them alive. And why do you have to do that? Because that's what you have to do.

[**Stimulates per- spective taking**]	*Karen:*	Who's to say you're the right person to decide?
	Mike:	The person who asked you to kill them.
[**Clarifies and summarizes the reasoning of the group**]	*Teacher:*	So you're saying a couple of things. The person has to want to die and someone who's close to him and who knows him very well has to agree that that's the best thing. [*Elements of stage 3*]

This shift in the teaching role toward a group-oriented perspective also means that the teacher can spend more time listening carefully to the stages of reasoning that students offer, and identify those that are *missing*. Listening gives the teacher greater assurance in knowing what the next higher level of cognitive complexity should be.

It is appropriate for the teacher to interject a personal opinion or moral argument once students are able to sustain the discussion themselves. Their own interest usually diminishes the concern that the teacher has "the right answer."

4. *Role-taking questions and strategies.* Role-taking questions are those specifically designed to stimulate students' perspective-taking ability. Role taking, of course, is part of most of the questioning strategies. In this section we specifically address the issue of stimulating students' perspectives from an egocentric level to one that considers the thoughts, feelings, and rights of others.

Role-taking opportunities are not restricted to discussions of moral problems. For students who are limited in their cognitive ability to take the role of others, actual experiences in assuming another person's role may be an important concrete link between their world and the world of others. Teachers need to develop cooperative activities for students at the elementary level. Role plays, debates, and student-designed plays, films, or slide tapes that center on moral conflicts also stimulate the real experience of walking in someone else's shoes. As in other questioning strategies, these activities are most beneficial when students focus on the *reasoning* the characters use as they enact the situation. This important addition to role plays (which usually stress personality and behavior) gives students the chance to "try on" another person's *thoughts* as well. This rehearsal can be a first step in moving beyond egocentric thinking. Discussing the role play afterward is also conducive to stimulating development, because this gives the whole class a chance to participate.

High school students can also benefit from real role-taking experiences. Taking the role of tutor to a younger child, or of a peer counselor to a fellow student, can help to develop students' perspective-taking capacity. The effort to help another person encourages the adolescent to see the world through that person's eyes.

In addition, role-taking opportunities occur during discussion when teachers ask certain questions. Leading discussions with adolescents whose role-taking ability is limited to egocentric reasoning is difficult because these adolescents have spent many more years in the preconventional pattern than younger children who reason at this level. Egocentric role taking must give way to a concern for others if an adolescent is to move from preconventional to conventional moral reasoning. One way to stimulate the beginnings of appreciation of others is to appeal to family ties. Affection and loyalty to people beyond oneself first develop in relation to the family.

The teacher in the example that follows demonstrates the importance of focusing on role taking when adolescents are at the preconventional level of moral reasoning. The teacher tries to follow the students' logic at their level of reasoning and at the same time to stimulate their ability to see beyond their own needs. This high school social studies class is discussing the legal and moral conflicts surrounding a gang of boys who steal cars. The class is exploring the issue of friendship as it relates to relationships in a gang. The dilemma and the topic of friendship are both appropriate content choices for stimulating moral development from the preconventional to the conventional level. One of the boys in the class has just defined a friend from the perspective of stage 2:

	Larry:	A friend is a friend as far as you can see him. . . . You know why I say a friend is a friend as far as you can trust him? You can go around stealing stuff [together] and all of a sudden he might just turn around and do it to you anyway. . . .
[Inter-issue probe]	*Teacher:*	Do you think trust is more important than staying out of jail?
	Ed:	Mmmm . . . depends on how much the other people mean to you, like whether you *want* them to trust you or not.
[Clarifying probe]	*Teacher:*	So it would make a difference to you if they were really your friends?
	John:	Of course. I'd probably tell in either situation but I'd be more reluctant if they were my friends.
	David:	I could get [i.e., give] a year in jail for my friends. It would be a problem, but I could give it up. [*Elements of stage 3*]
[Asks question to highlight contiguous stage arguments]	*Teacher:*	Would you turn your friends in, Larry?
	Larry:	All depends if I like him. Or if I wanted to see him suffer. . . . [*Elements of stage 2*]
[Role-taking appeal to family ties]	*Teacher:*	Larry, what if the person who had to turn you in was your brother?
	Larry:	I wouldn't rat on my brother.

[Issue-specific probe]	*Teacher:*	What is the difference?
	John:	Oh, I can't do that if it was my brother. I couldn't tell on my brother.
[Issue-specific probe]	*Teacher:*	What makes your brother different from a friend?
	John:	Blood. Blood is thicker than water. Even if I really disliked my brother or hated him I couldn't tell on him. Blood is thicker than water. [*Elements of stage 3*]
	Paul:	I'm not so sure. I wouldn't go up and tell the police if it was my brother, but if I was in a painful situation and the police were pressuring me I wouldn't think it would be wrong to tell. It's not my fault. It's my brother that got himself into trouble and it is his fault. [*Elements of stage 2*]

In this excerpt we see the teacher taking active responsibility for introducing a broader frame of reference *and* encouraging other students with different perspectives to interact together. Theoretically, the most effective kind of cognitive stimulation from a developmental standpoint is a comment or question (by either student or teacher) at a *slightly* more complex level of perspective taking. The teacher did not ask the students what people in society would think if everyone thought as the students did. That question would be more stimulating to students who were already able to take the perspective of a group of friends. Rather, the adult first clarified the students' concept of friendship in order to take their perspective. Then he presented the first possible perspective available beyond their own, that of their family: "What if the person who had to turn you in was your brother? . . . What makes your brother different from a friend?" It was equally important for the teacher to help Larry and Paul hear what John and David had to say about friendship, since they demonstrate the ability to take a perspective that incorporates notions of trust, loyalty, and obligation to others—which are characteristic of mutual role taking at stage 3.

The importance of the four in-depth questioning strategies is that they heighten cognitive conflict and extend students' role-taking ability. Although we have stressed particular questions here to illustrate the cognitive conflict-inducing process necessary over time to produce restructuring of moral reasoning, it is important to note that such questioning takes place within the context of a discussion. Discussion among students ultimately enables students to be exposed to various levels of reasoning and requires that each student formulate or construct a reasoned response in dialogue. Such construction, motivated by the need to respond to one's peers, as well as to the teacher, helps create the conditions for moral development.

A cautionary word about classroom discussion is in order here. As mentioned earlier, research data have shown that discussion programs can stimulate moral growth, but such programs are generally not part of the larger curriculum and have only a limited effect on the student's overall education. Perhaps it would be wise to restate Kohlberg's view of classroom discussion in the context of a moral education program:

> If brief periods of classroom discussion can have a substantial effect on moral development, a pervasive, enduring and psychologically sound concern for the school's influence upon moral development should have much deeper effects. Such a concern would pervade the curriculum areas of social studies, law education, philosophy and sex education, rather than representing a new curriculum area. More deeply, it would affect the social atmosphere and justice structure of the school.[7]

HIDDEN CURRICULUM

There is much that goes on in schools alongside formal learning. Schools are places in which students and teachers spend a good part of their time five days a week, ten months a year. As social institutions, schools are characterized by what Philip Jackson has called the crowds, the praise, and the power. Students have to learn to live as members of a crowd of peers; they have to work hard to gain the praise and avoid the censure of their peers and teachers; and they have to learn to abide by or artfully dodge the rule and authority structure set up by the school system. Students learn a great deal about social behavior and moral values from this "hidden curriculum," perhaps more than they do from the formal curriculum.

Kohlberg believes that the hidden curriculum offers a rich opportunity for educators to involve students in moral learning. In this regard Kohlberg's work evidences the same concerns for learning how to care for, and consider, others and the potential moral learning from peers that McPhail discusses. And although students can learn much from reading about and discussing social and moral issues, there is no substitute for participating in real-life social and moral issues. Because such issues arise naturally within the context of school life, Kohlberg suggests using the opportunities for involving students in this deliberation. Why only teach about democracy when one can also practice democracy within the context of the school? Kohlberg, like Shaver, pays great attention to the notion of education within and for a democracy. And like the social action model of moral education, discussed in chapter 8, Kohlberg's model has an action or behavior component. This dimension is described as the creation of a "just community" school.

THE JUST COMMUNITY APPROACH [8]

This approach proposes that in the implementation of developmental moral education, a conducive classroom atmosphere should be set up. Moral issues should be raised to awareness and considered in classroom discussions. Probing questions should be used to stimulate cognitive conflict. Single discussions should be woven into the curriculum and used as means for resolving conflicts that arise within the classroom. Moral issues do not end at the classroom's door, however. They often involve the school as a whole or, at least, larger units within the school. If there are racial or social-class tensions, incidents of stealing and vandalism, people who are dissatisfied with the academic policy or with the way the lunchroom is run, the source of the problems lies not in single classrooms but in the school. Schools as well as classrooms have moral atmospheres, and although it is much harder to change whole schools, some problems can be dealt with only on a school-wide level.

We are not yet aware of a large school that has attempted to alter its structure in the light of Kohlberg's theory. Nevertheless, there have been efforts to create alternative "schools within a school" that incorporate aspects of the theory. Kohlberg has been involved with one such alternative high school in Cambridge, Massachusetts.

He and his colleagues are attempting to implement a "just community" approach to moral education. The school began in 1974 and involves sixty to seventy students (in ninth to twelfth grades) and six staff members. At the heart of the school's operation is a concern for democratic governance and opportunities for moral discussions arising out of the daily routine of school life.

The school began in September, 1974, with about sixty students and six staff members who volunteered to participate. The school met in two adjacent classrooms within Cambridge High School. Students were required to take a daily two-hour core course in English and social studies; elective courses were also offered, but students took many of their courses in the regular school. The staff divided its time between working in the alternative and regular schools. Thus both staff and students retained a dual status as members of both schools.

Democratic Governance

Democratic governance stands at the heart of the just community approach. For students and teachers to overcome their reliance on traditional authority patterns, they have to learn to democratically share the responsibility for decision making.

Traditionally, teachers and administrators make decisions in the school. They claim the power for themselves and are left with the responsibility for enforcing their decisions and rules. They may or may not take time to explain to students the rationale for these decisions; in either event, they expect students to abide by the rules whether or not they understand or agree with them. Students are left with the choice of either passively obeying, actively rejecting, or subtly undermining the staff's decisions.

Even though this traditional authority pattern may prove relatively effective from a managerial perspective, from the perspective of moral development theory there is little to recommend it. Passive acceptance or a negative rejection are not stances that are likely to promote students' moral development. Insofar as students stand outside the decision-making process, they will not feel responsible for decisions that are made. They will not see themselves as *morally* bound to uphold rules, but only as *pragmatically* bound to conform or avoid punishment.

The Cambridge alternative school is run as a direct democracy. Everyone in the school meets once a week for a two-hour community meeting at which basic decisions about how to run the school are made. Although the rules of the larger school are in effect, the community exercises the right to interpret these rules and enforce them in its own way. Thus, cutting classes or using drugs is outlawed in the larger school, but in the alternative school these rules were adopted by the community only after intensive discussion when a majority agreed to their necessity. Initially the community voted a liberal policy of allowing everyone ten legal cuts, far more than was allowed in Cambridge High School. When that policy interfered with the running of classes, the community altered its course and allowed no legal cuts. That proved unenforceable, and so a compromise of four cuts was adopted. At meetings, the teachers spoke for allowing fewer cuts, but it was the majority of students who made the decision.

The students also enforce decisions. No one gets sent to the headmaster or has to see the teacher after class. Violators of rules are responsible to the community. Initially the students were reluctant to discipline one another, but when it became clear to them that classes could not be conducted smoothly when too many students were disruptive or absent, they began disciplining peers who were guilty of excessive behavior. Their investment in their own learning and in the maintenance of the school overcame their reluctance to punish peers.

A democratically run community meeting for seventy or eighty people is a hard show to run. It requires a number of requisite conditions: (1) that the students' interest be maintained; (2) that there is a clear but flexible procedural order; (3) that issues are raised clearly, and the pros and cons of concrete proposals can be discussed; (4) that students and staff discuss the issues by voicing reasons for their stands and avoid attacking one another on personal grounds; (5) that everyone feels that the decisions of the community will be carried out and will not be subverted by higher authorities or dissenting minorities.

In the Cambridge school, none of these conditions was present in the fall of 1974. There was no established procedural order and the staff ran the meetings. Students spoke up far less than did staff, and when students did voice an opinion, it was unsupported by any reasons. Votes were called precipitously. Students were distrustful of the faculty and used their majority to vote for decisions like dismissing school early. Only gradually, over a year's time, did the conditions listed above come into existence.

Once the community started making decisions and adopting rules, it was expected that both staff and students would adhere to them. Adherence has not always been forthcoming, however. To deal with violations of its rules, the community has set up a rotating discipline committee made up of one student representative from each small group and two staff members. If, for example, a student disrupts a class or is caught using drugs, or a faculty member is accused of acting abusively to a student, the case comes before the committee at its weekly meeting. If the person involved is a first-time offender, the committee tries to effect a reconciliation between the parties. If there has been a history of offense, the committee recommends a punishment to the community. The community hears the case, allows the parties to present their sides, discusses the issues, and makes its decision. Often the offender is given every chance to make amends and change his ways; but when that route has been exhausted, parents have been called and students expelled from the school.

Kohlberg considers this way of running a school to be "just" not only because it is directly democratic but also because the community's decisions can be made at the highest level of moral reasoning available to its student members. That is not to say at a principled level, for no students in this school have developed beyond stage 4, and most reason at a stage 3 level. The staff's task is not to impose higher-stage reasoning but to offer the soundest reasoning students are capable of understanding and to continually encourage students to exercise the best of their moral reasoning in arriving at communal decisions. When that is achieved, and when students stand behind their decisions and enforce them, the school can be said to be operating as a just community.

The Cambridge School in Action

To give a more concrete sense of this school in operation, let us consider how the community dealt with the problem of stealing in its first two years.

Students' stealing property from others is a common problem in Cambridge, as it is in many high schools. In December of the first year, an intern working at the alternative school invited a group of students to her home to make candles. The next day, her roommate told her five pairs of earrings were missing. Since there had been no other guests or intruders, they suspected a student had taken them. But when the intern raised the issue at school, no one would volunteer any information.

A month later, a student brought to school a box of silver rings, which he showed around. During class, one of the rings "disappeared." All anyone would say was that the ring had been pushed out the window.

As a result of these incidents, the issue of stealing was raised at a January community meeting. The meeting opened with a proposal from one group that "the people who stole should go to the discipline committee and the property should be returned or paid for." There was some discussion as to what the punishment would be, but nothing more happened until the staff interceded. Kohlberg, who has participated regularly in these meetings, asked: "Maybe someone can explain why the stealing has been going on. Don't people think it is wrong and a violation of the community?"

Student reaction was subdued. One student responded: "I don't think you should worry about that. The fact is it happened, and to worry about why it happened isn't worth it."

But the staff persisted: "I think that ripping off is not an individual business; it is a community business. It is not a discipline issue as much as it is some feeling by the community that people have to have a level of trust which is inconsistent with anybody ripping off from anybody else in the community."

Only one student picked up on the level of trust; the sentiments of the majority were expressed by a frank girl who said: "This is a bunch of bull. You can make a rule [about stealing], but everyone doesn't have to get upset. . . . Someone is always on your back in this school."

The discussion returned to making a rule about stealing. Although no one was sure it would work, all agreed that making a rule and stipulating a punishment for its violation was a first step. As one student argued: "If they call his parents about it, next time he will think about it and it will cut down on it."

With that argument the meeting ended, but the problem persisted. Stealing continued throughout the first year and in the beginning of the school's second year.

In October of the second year, nine dollars was taken from the purse of one of the female students. She was pretty certain that a student had taken the money, but no one would admit to it. A community meeting was called to discuss the incident.

The reports from the small groups that opened the meeting reflected a concern on the students' part that acts like stealing were disruptive to their sense of community: "We said that everybody give fifteen cents because fifteen cents isn't going to hurt you." That is, if every member gave fifteen cents, the nine dollars could be returned to the student from whom it was stolen. The rationale for this collective reimbursement was interesting:

> Everyone, some fifty people, should put in fifteen cents to give her back her money because it is not her fault. It is everybody's fault, because people just don't care about the community. [They think] they are all individuals and don't have to be involved in the community. [But] everybody should care that she got her money stolen.

This statement by a student and the support it received from other students marked a turning point in the school's development toward a just community. For the first time, students articulated a sense that they were responsible for what went on in the school. That if someone's money were stolen, it was everyone's fault for not caring enough about the community. To be sure, the statement was challenged by students who felt that the theft was the responsibility of either the girl who allowed her money to be stolen or the individual who stole the money. But the majority agreed to a compromise proposal that if the money were not returned by a certain date, every member would pay fifteen cents to reimburse the money.

That this was a turning point was borne out by events that followed the meeting. For a week there was no confession, and it seemed that everyone would have to pay. Then some students admitted they knew who stole the money and agreed to speak to the guilty person privately. When this proved unsuccessful, they grew impatient with the person and revealed her name to the group. Eventually she was expelled by her peers from the school. More important was the fact that there were no further incidents of stealing in the school. Students did not swear off stealing entirely, but came to an agreement articulated by one student at the meeting: "If you want to rip off, rip off on your own time and not in school."

The progress from first to second year, as reflected in these meetings, was modest, but significant. We can understand it in the following terms:

1. The students took a more active role in the second year in dealing with stealing as a community problem. They made the connection that they could not have a community if people could not trust one another with their property.

2. The quality of the meeting improved, for students not only proposed different actions but also backed up their proposals with reasoning about why they should be adopted. Students addressed one another's positions and reasons.

3. A decision was made that led from judgment to action. Whereas in the first year rules and punishment did not deter stealing, in the second year a norm evolved among students that stealing was not to take place in the school. Their revealing the name of the person who stole meant they would be willing to enforce this norm.

The progress was modest. In a neighborhood with a lot of street theft, one cannot expect to eliminate all stealing at once. Nevertheless, an important inroad was made, not only because the students all agreed not to steal in school, but also because they became attached enough to an institution to care about upholding its norms. We believe that their active role in forming the norm was essential to their committing themselves to its enforcement.

SUMMARY AND APPRAISAL

The formation of a community as a process for involving students in the moral deliberations of determining school policy is a complex and time-consuming process. It requires a commitment to cognitive moral development as an essential goal of schooling. At this point in time Kohlberg's notion of "just community" is the leading edge of his moral education theory. Research is at present being conducted to determine if student "immersion" into the hidden moral life of the school adds power to the earlier moral discussion results.

The strength of Kohlberg's work derives from the fact that he has integrated philosophy, psychology, and pedagogy such that the rationale for practice has a sound theoretical base on which to begin. One of the major strengths of the cognitive moral development model is that it focuses full attention on moral issues, on the resolution of particular value conflicts. Further, the developmental approach acknowledges the complexity of human growth and that social factors and time are powerful ingredients in moral learning. Yet, both theoretical and practical problems exist.

Some critics have suggested that Kohlberg's philosophy of morality represents a Western cultural bias and wonder if such a theory of justice as morality can lay claim to being universal. Others question the validity of Kohlberg's cross-cultural research methodology and for this reason question the claim for the universal nature of the stages of moral development. The debate on these matters will continue until a significant number of further cross-cultural and longitudinal studies are reported.

In a more practical domain, the model also causes problems. Teachers poorly trained in the theory are inclined to misuse the stages of development by labeling their students. Typing children in this way is an insidious albeit unintended side effect of the model.

Related to the labeling issue is the problem of evaluation. How does the teacher know if there has been a restructuring of moral reasoning? Because our schools are so oriented toward "measurable" growth, teachers may find it frustrating to embrace a model that involves long-term learning (often up to five years) and is difficult to measure precisely.

Teachers may also become frustrated by the nature of the teaching model inherent in Kohlberg's work. Whereas teachers are more normally oriented to providing students with information and "right" answers, and to resolving inter- and intrapersonal conflict, they may find it difficult to become stimulators of cognitive conflict. That is, the theory demands that students be confronted at their present level of thinking by a conflicting point of view. This leads to some student discomfort, and the need for both students and teacher to live with a degree of ambiguity not previously experienced. Many teachers feel uncomfortable with such a conflict-inducing role.

Kohlberg's model focuses a great deal of attention on reasoning. While the theory also takes into account the roles of emotion and behavior, the linkages among all three are not sufficiently clear. Kohlberg's latest research regarding the development and effects of learning in a just community may begin to tie these aspects together.

In summary, Kohlberg's work incorporates many of the issues raised by previous models: a strong rationale for moral education within the context of democracy; sensitizing students to their own and others' moral values; resolving moral conflict through the use of reason; considering the rights, points of view, and feelings of others; and a concern for linking reasoning, emotion, and behavior. This model provides the most comprehensive philosophical and psychological rationale, but its application in schools may be enhanced by incorporating many of the strategies provided in the alternative models provided in this book.

REFERENCES

Principal Source

Hersh, Richard; Diana Paolitto; and Joseph Reimer. *Promoting Moral Growth: From Piaget to Kohlberg.* New York: Longman, 1979.

Related Sources

Fenton, Edwin, and Lawrence Kohlberg. *Teacher Training in Values Education.* New York: Guidance Associates, 1977.
This is a sound-filmstrip kit designed to provide teacher training in Kohlberg's approach. The principal focus is on developing classroom discussion skills.

Kohlberg, Lawrence. *Collected Papers on Moral Development and Moral Education.* Cambridge, Mass.: Harvard Graduate School of Education, Spring, 1973.
An excellent collection of Kohlberg's papers. The emphasis is theoretical but practical applications are also discussed.

Kohlberg, Lawrence, and Robert Selman. *First Things: Values.* New York: Guidance Associates, 1972.
A set of sound filmstrips that present dilemmas for use in the elementary school classroom. A teacher-training filmstrip and guide are included.

Ladenburg, Thomas; Muriel Ladenburg; and Peter Scharf. *Moral Education: A Classroom Workbook.* Davis, Calif.: Responsible Action, 1978.
A collection of moral dilemmas for use in the classroom. Model lesson plans are provided.

Mattox, Beverly A. *Getting It Together: Dilemmas for the Classroom.* San Diego, Calif.: Pennant, 1975.
A set of dilemmas for elementary and secondary school levels.

Pagluiso, Susan. *Understanding Stages of Moral Development: A Programmed Learning Workbook.* New York: Paulist Press, 1976.

Piaget, Jean. *Moral Judgment of the Child.* New York: Collier, 1962.

Scharf, Peter. *Moral Education.* Davis, Calif.: Responsible Action, 1978.
A review of theories of moral development and their implications for curriculum design and classroom practice.

Selman, Robert, et al. *First Things: Social Reasoning.* New York: Guidance Associates, 1974.

8
THE SOCIAL ACTION MODEL

The social action model of moral education developed by Fred Newmann integrates several dimensions discussed in previous chapters and relates them to citizen involvement in social change. For example, the model discusses the importance of group discussion skills, various affective issues such as trust and commitment, and the necessity for moral reasoning skills. The approach aims to teach students how to influence public policy.

Some of the approaches examined in earlier chapters have action components. Lawrence Kohlberg, for example, developed the just community school, a setting that emphasizes moral action. A basic component of the values clarification process is acting in a reasonably consistent manner with one's values. In only the Newmann model, however, is the primary focus on citizen action. Instead of encouraging "reflection" on or "taking an active interest" in public matters, the Newmann approach emphasizes the right of each citizen to exert an influence on public affairs. Newmann argues that in the past, citizenship education has not dealt with effective action but has focused on other facets of citizenship.

One such emphasis has been on academic disciplines. Students have gained knowledge about history and the social sciences. Another focus has been on the legal-political structure of government. Courses in civics and law have informed students about formal aspects of the system. A third emphasis has been on social issues like war, crime, and poverty. A fourth has emphasized the intellectual processes of reaching sound conclusions. Students have studied logical inference, the validation of empirical claims, the consistency of argument, and propaganda. The assumption has been that learning these analytic skills will transfer to participation in the democratic process.[1]

In general, these approaches have reinforced citizen passivity. To counter this passivity the Newmann approach does not emphasize activity per se; instead, the basic aim is *environmental competence*. Environmental competence involves action to effect specific consequences on the environment. Newmann feels that civic education has focused mostly on self-oriented projects (i.e., clarifying personal values) rather than the development of competence. Environmental competence can be broken down as follows:

A.   Physical—ability to have an impact on objects
  1. Aesthetic (painting a picture)
  2. Functional (building a house)
B.   Interpersonal—ability to have impact on persons
  1. Nurturing relationships (caring for a baby or friend)
  2. Economic relationships (selling a car)
C.   Civic—ability to have an impact in public affairs
  1. Public electoral process (helping a candidate win election)
  2. Within interest groups (changing policy priorities of a consumer protection group)[2]

The focus of the social action model is on the last category: civic action.

THEORY

Why pursue environmental competence? Newmann brings up several points in support of a program in citizen action.

Morality

Newmann suggests a direct relationship between the ability to exert influence on the environment and the degree to which persons can consider themselves moral agents. Newmann defines a moral agent as "someone who deliberates upon what he or she ought to do in situations that involve possible conflicts between self interests and the interests of others, or between the rights of parties in conflict." [3] Unfortunately, many young people do not feel they can affect the environment and thus are not interested in moral questions.

Students may perceive injustice regarding the environment, civil rights, and economic exploitation. Because they feel they cannot influence these matters, however, they do not see them as relevant to their lives. If moral issues are to have meaning, the individual must feel that he or she can affect the problem in some manner. A sense of environmental competence is integral to the development of moral sensibility.

Psychological Development

Not only is the ability to influence the environment important if one wishes to be a moral agent but it is essential to one's psychological development. Newmann refers to the work of Robert White, whose research supports the notion that much of human behavior is explainable by the need to feel competent. (This contrasts with the belief that most human activity is an attempt to cope with basic instinctual drives.) The ability to gain a sense of competence is integral to the development of ego strength or "the ability to overcome anxiety associated with perceived 'dangers' or 'threats' because of the accrued confidence that one can act upon, rather than be a victim of, the environment." [4]

Consent of the Governed

The consent of the governed requires that each "citizen has an equal opportunity to affect the use of power; through periodic selection of leaders and through direct participation to affect the outcome of specific issues." [5] The consent of the governed attempts to ensure that equal rights are not violated and that ideas and policies are tested in the public arena. Low levels of citizen participation endanger this principle. When general participation is low, special-interest groups can control or manipulate the political process. The Newmann program is based on the premise that developing social action skills can improve the democratic process by facilitating the consent of the governed. "Social action" is not meant to imply militant forms of protest but is construed more generally to take in all behavior directed toward exerting an influence in public affairs. Social action can thus include

> telephone conversations, letter writing, participation in meetings, research and study, testifying before public bodies, door-to-door canvassing, fund-raising media production, bargaining and negotiation; and also publicly visible activity associated with the more militant forms. Social action can take place in or out of school and, if out of school, not necessarily in the streets, but in homes, offices, and workplaces. It might involve movement among several locations or concentration at one.[6]

To qualify as social action, however, the above activities must be part of a strategy to influence public policy in a particular direction. Issues can vary:

> Students may wish to work for better bicycle trails, improved low-income housing, a "freer" school, the opening of a drug counseling center, the election of a particular official. They might wish to oppose a curfew ordinance, high-rise apartments, credit practices of a particular firm, or a school's dress code.[7]

Newmann suggests that environmental competence should be an important aim of the school, but other competencies should not be ignored. Nonetheless, he makes a strong case for citizen action as the priority that should not be sacrificed or subordinated to other objectives.

The major components of the Newmann model are outlined in figure 8.1. The first step in the model is to formulate policy goals based on moral deliberation and social policy research. Having formulated goals (e.g., the repeal of anti-abortion laws), the citizen gathers support to implement the goals. This involves knowledge of the political process, advocacy skills, group-process skills, and management skills. Involvement in citizen action may also bring to the surface definite psychophilosophic concerns that must be dealt with. The results of the overall process are the actual policy outcomes.

Figure 8.1. Areas of Competence Required to Exert Influence in Public Affairs

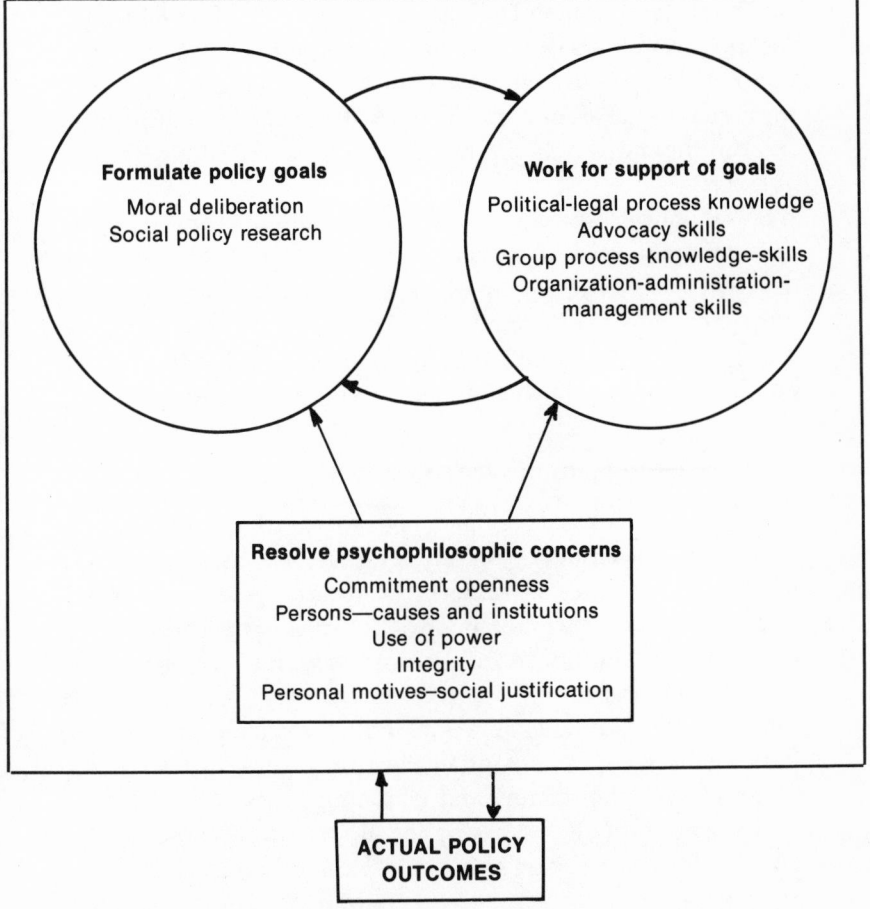

Source: Fred W. Newmann, *Education for Citizen Action: Challenge for Secondary Curriculum* (Berkeley, Calif.: McCutchan, 1975), p. 77.

Formulating Policy Goals

There are two basic components to the task of formulating policy goals: moral deliberation and social policy research.

In moral deliberation, Newmann suggests that individuals must be prepared to engage in reasoned, open debate concerning their policies and principles. Rational argument should be combined with substantive values to bring about effective moral deliberation. In short, Newmann rejects ethical relativism and adopts the position (similar to Kohlberg's) that some values or principles (e.g., the right to life) should hold priority over others (e.g., the right to property). Newmann recognizes that values compete with one another and that only through rational argument and commitment to substantive values can the moral deliberation process lead to ethically justifiable goals.

Social policy research attempts to ascertain the consequences of certain policies. The student examines the possible effects of different social action alternatives (e.g., the effects of interracial busing on pupil achievement). Such research sometimes produces tentative and conflicting findings because the individual often has to make conclusions based on limited information.

Working for Support of One's Goals

After someone has developed a position through moral deliberation and social policy research, he or she must engage in a number of activities to achieve the desired goals. The social activist must become familiar with the "rules of the game." This involves knowing how a bill becomes law, how decisions can be appealed, and so forth. Equally important is knowing about informal, less public channels of influence: for example, key individuals who are potential allies or groups that have resources in people, money, and bargaining power.

Equally important in working for support are advocacy skills. These skills relate to one's ability to plead a cause in a systematic and rational manner. Advocacy skills also involve arguing the case so that people can identify with the message and respond emotionally and cognitively to the position.

As an individual begins to work for support, group-process knowledge and skills are also important. This dimension involves decisions about whether a person should join an existing organization or form a new group. If a new group is formed, it demands consideration of such issues as membership, internal authority, and division of responsibility. Knowledge of interpersonal behavior in groups is also a consideration. This means learning what helps and what hinders group functioning, as well as how to integrate this knowledge into interpersonal behavior. For example, instruction could be offered in listening skills, seeking clarification of other group members' ideas and feelings, summarizing individual contributions to form a group position, and giving and receiving feedback in an honest and open group.

Finally, organization-management skills are necessary. For example:

> When is the right time for door-to-door canvassing? Would a mail or phone campaign be more effective? How soon should we contact the press and what should we tell them? Could we raise more funds through a bake sale or by soliciting special donations? Should we accept the man's word or press him to sign a statement? [8]

Newmann suggests that the skills needed in working for support provide a broad agenda for curriculum development. It would be unreasonable to expect, however, that students would become competent in all the skills mentioned above.

Resolving Psychophilosophic Concerns

As a person becomes involved in social action, a number of concerns can arise. Newmann identifies these concerns as psychophilosophic dilemmas. They must be faced if the individual is to become effective in citizen action.

One such concern involves commitment and openness. This means developing the appropriate balance between being committed to a project and keeping a reasonable amount of openness to constructive criticism. The danger here is that people can become obsessive about their commitments or, conversely, can be so open to suggestion that their commitment becomes ambivalent.

Another dilemma involves a consideration of persons versus causes or institutions. Sometimes individuals become so involved in a project or cause that their adversaries become objects to be defeated or blamed. It is essential that individuals retain a sense of compassion toward everyone involved in an action project. Nevertheless, it is also important that activists not forget the overall purpose of the activity and not become overly responsive to others' needs.

Related to human responsiveness is the issue of individual integrity. At times during a social action project, a person can be faced with choices that can compromise his or her basic integrity. The willingness to compromise is important, but there are limits to how far anyone should modify a position. When a decision compromises an individual's basic values and identity, he or she may have to examine alternative approaches.

The individual must also examine the use of power in the project. For example, who will be the leader and who the followers? The one who emerges as leader must be careful not to abuse the leadership role. The person with the responsibility to make decisions also will find that power can "hurt" others. If an organization has limited funds and can have only one staff member, the leader may have to turn away some well-qualified applicants.

A final issue that may arise in social action projects is the relationship between personal motives and social justifications. It is important for people to be aware of their motives in pursuing a social action project. Newmann has discovered the following motives among students involved in citizen action: self-education, task completion, recreation, and hibernation. Sometimes the personal motive may conflict with the overall project. For example, a student whose basic motive is to learn about the political process may not want to do clerical work for a candidate because the student could learn more by participating in higher-lever discussions. This could conflict with the goal of winning the election. Conflicts such as this must be examined by the student before he or she decides on a role in the project.

Although Newmann has broken his model into a number of components, he does not advocate developing individual skills and competencies at the expense of cooperation and collective action.

PRACTICE

Newmann has implemented his approach in a secondary school course, the Community Issues Program, in Madison, Wisconsin. As for implementing the program in other settings, Newmann suggests the relationship between the social action components and subjects in the secondary school curriculum shown in table 8.1. Ideally, a sequential sequence could be constructed. Newmann offers the following approach:

1st Semester: Political-legal process course
               Communications course
               Community service internship
2nd Semester: Citizen action project
               Action in literature project
               Public message [9]

The competencies to be developed in these courses include

1. Communicate effectively in spoken and written language
2. Collect and logically interpret information on problems of public concern
3. Describe political-legal decision-making processes
4. Rationally justify personal decisions on controversial public issues and strategies for action with reference to principles of justice and constitutional democracy
5. Work cooperatively with others
6. Discuss concrete personal experiences of self and others in ways that contribute to resolution of personal dilemmas encountered in civic action and that relate these experiences to more general human issues
7. Use selected technical skills as they are required for exercise of influence on specific issues [10]

The curriculum includes a year-long program in which students would spend almost full-time (e.g., 9:30 A.M. to 2:00

TABLE 8.1. RELATIONSHIP OF SOCIAL ACTION COMPONENTS TO SUBJECTS IN THE CURRICULUM

Social Action Component	Subject Covered	Additional Subjects That Could Contribute
Moral deliberation	Social studies [a] (English)	Philosophy Literature
Social policy research	Social studies (sciences, math)	Any subject relevant to the policy under consideration
Political-legal process	Social studies	Law Sociology
Advocacy	English (speech, journalism)	Law Public relations History
Group process	English Psychology	Sociology Social psychology Community organization
Organization-administration-management	None	Business management Accounting Labor relations
Psychophilosophic concerns	None	History Philosophy Literature (biography) Religion Psychology Counseling

Source: Fred W. Newmann, *Education for Citizen Action: Challenge for Secondary Curriculum* (Berkeley, Calif.: McCutchan, 1975), p. 113.
[a] Social studies refers collectively to history and the many social science disciplines (sociology, anthropology, political science, psychology, economics, etc.).

P.M.). They would earn two credits in English and two credits in social studies and would have time to take an additional course in math, science, or a foreign language. Newmann and his associates also recommend that the program be open to about sixty students and run by two full-time teachers. The courses in the program are described in the following paragraphs.

1. *Political-legal process course,* three mornings a week, for fourteen weeks, during the first semester. Here the student

would learn the "realities" of the political system. There would be an examination of the formal structure of the system, as well as of informal processes like lobbying and bargaining. Students would also have "firsthand" opportunities to observe these processes in action through field experiences. These experiences could involve attending meetings and conducting interviews. The course could also focus on developing skills in data gathering and drawing valid conclusions. Moral deliberation skills (see chapter 7) would also be dealt with in this part of the program, and the student would have the opportunity to develop position papers on controversial issues.

2. *Communications course,* four afternoons a week, for sixteen weeks, during the first semester. Here the student would develop skills in written, spoken, and nonverbal communications. Skills would be applied to four contexts: intrapersonal, interpersonal, group, and the public. For example, the student could work on interpersonal helping skills such as empathy and regard, as well as group skills such as problem identification and clarification. Emphasis would also be given to building trust and group cohesion so that the student could work with others.

3. *Community service internship,* two mornings a week, for fourteen weeks, during the first semester. Students would be involved in volunteer work in social agencies, government bodies, and public interest groups.

The intern might work in an understudy relationship to one adult for the entire period (e.g., as an aide to a TV news reporter), might have short tours of duty among different groups (e.g., helping in several different departments in an environmental protection agency), might be involved in special projects (e.g., gathering data for a neighborhood organization), might offer direct social services to "clients" (e.g., tutoring young children or assisting the elderly). The placement should expose the student to the daily functioning of the agency, should provide opportunities for the student to communicate actively with agency people (rather than passively observe them), and should require that the student make a contribution to the agency's mission. [11]

As the students become involved in internship, they could analyze institutional processes of the agency in the political-legal process course and work on relevant language skills in the communications course. One afternoon per week, students could "share their volunteer experiences, discuss common problems, and begin to explore issues that might develop into the citizen action project for the second semester." [12]

4. *Citizenship action project*, four mornings a week, for ten weeks, during the second semester. In this part of the program the students would work to affect public policy.

> Projects could involve working for political candidates, establish-ment of special youth institutions, revision of administrative regula-tions, lobbying for legislation, etc. The issues could concern na-tional, state, or local agencies, including the schools; for example, student rights within a school, zoning provisions to protect the en-vironment, consumer protection, interracial cooperation, improved social services for youth in trouble. [13]

The project could develop from the first semester's work. Dur-ing the project the students could also take "skill clinics" on such matters as canvassing techniques, negotiation skills, fund raising, and how to run a meeting. "Project counseling ses-sions" would also be offered to deal with various issues that arise during the project and would provide psychological sup-port to the students.

5. *Action in literature project*, two afternoons a week, for ten weeks, during the second semester. This course has a more general focus than the others and deals with such issues as What is meaningful social change? Can an individual make a difference? and How should humans govern themselves? These questions can be pursued through fiction, biography, poetry, and drama. For example, students might read a biography on Gandhi, Thoreau on civil disobedience, a novel such as *All the King's Men*, and the work of James Baldwin.

6. *Public message*. Each citizen action group would develop a final "message" on their activities to be shared with their peers and the public at large. Students would study the various media and prepare a report on their activities for one of these media.

The emphasis would be on what had been accomplished in the project and aim to interpret the students' experience to the public.

Newmann recommends the overall program be open to students in grades eleven and twelve. Although social action programs should rate a high priority, it is suggested that actual course work not be required for all students because this would constitute an unjustified restriction on students' freedom. Newmann also indicates that not enough research has been done to be certain about program outcomes. Finally, it is also recommended that student self-selection be used in choosing students for the program. The main objective—environmental competence—should be strongly publicized so that students are aware of the purpose of the course.

Student Projects

Three community-involvement projects are identified for the program. "In exploratory research students investigate the community, gathering information through field trips, interviews, guest speakers, informal observation in community institutions, and other means." [14] Volunteer service places the student in a direct helping relationship to others. For example, students work in homes for the elderly, day-care centers, tutoring programs, and neighborhood clean-up campaigns. Social action projects ask the student to take an advocate position and attempt to affect change congruent with that position. Newmann suggests that a developmental relationship might exist with the three projects. Exploratory research is more self-oriented as the individual goes into the community to gather relevant information. Volunteer service involves more participation as the individual may help or care for others. Finally, in the advocacy role, students emerge as autonomous agents who engage in concerns that relate to a broader social context.

Although the advocacy role is seen as the most congruent with the aim of environmental competence, the other projects are legitimate components of a social action program. Newmann recommends that a tangible product be developed during the activity. A list of competences and products are shown in table 8.2.

TABLE 8.2. DATA TO DOCUMENT STUDENT PROFICIENCY AND PRODUCTIVITY ON SEVEN CITIZEN ACTION COMPETENCIES

Competency	Data	
	Proficiency	Productivity
1. Communicate effectively in spoken and written language.	Objective tests in vocabulary, written, media analysis. Evaluative testimony from teacher and others on written work and oral presentations. Exhibits such as book reports, research studies, letters, scripts, journal.	Inventory of the number and types of communication produced (letters, reports, speeches, minutes, interviews, brochures).
2. Collect and logically interpret information on problems of public concern.	Objective tests in data interpretation (e.g., graphs and tables) and location (where would you find the following information in this community or elsewhere?). Teacher evaluation of position statements—oral and written.	Inventory of research tasks completed in political-legal process course, internship, action project, public message.
3. Describe political-legal decision-making processes.	Objective tests on local government and institutions salient in the internship and action project. Testimony from teachers and others on students' ability to plan appropriate strategies. Logs or student histories of particular decisions.	Inventory of experiences with different parts and people in the political-legal system.

4. Rationally justify personal decisions or controversial public issues and strategies for action with reference to principles of justice and constitutional democracy.	Tests on skills in identifying issues, and applying principles of justice (e.g., equality) and constitutional democracy (e.g., due process of majority rule). Testimony from teachers and others written and oral attempts to take a stand on controversial issues. Exhibits of position papers, speeches.	Inventory of number and types of positions taken orally and in writing.
5. Work cooperatively with others.	Objective tests on ability to analyze group behavior. Testimony from teacher peers and others on specific cooperative behaviors. Self-analysis of group skills. Exhibit of group projects.	Inventory of number and types group efforts and types of contributions made.
6. Discuss concrete personal experience of self and others in ways that contribute to resolution of personal dilemmas of citizenship and that explore more general human issues.	Tests on translating specific experiences into more general issues. Teacher testimony on students' oral and written analysis of literature and personal action work. Exhibits such as student essays, diaries, tape-recordings, completed public message.	Inventory of activities completed where this was the goal (e.g., counseling sessions, discussion of literature, rap sessions at the internship of action project).
7. Use selected technical skills as required for the exercise of influence on specific issues.	Objective tests and testimony from experts on particular skills such as photography, canvassing, parliamentary procedures.	Inventory of occasions in which skills were used.

Source: Fred Newmann, Thomas Bertocci, and Ruthanne M. Landsness, *Skills in Citizen Action: An English–Social Studies Program for Secondary Schools* (Skokie, Ill.: National Textbook, 1977), pp. 119–20.

The creation of the product encourages a more systematic approach to the project than merely "having an experience." The products also assist in the evaluation process.

Evaluation of the program focuses on four areas: (1) proficiency, or the mastery of knowledge and skills related to citizen action; (2) productivity, which emphasizes the importance of completing the project; (3) persistence, which refers to taking the project seriously and becoming fully engaged in the activity; and pleasurability, or the amount of enjoyment the student gets from the program. The staff and students should not expect that all criteria will apply all the time, but they should come to some mutually agreed-upon priorities with respect to program criteria. Evaluation of the four *p*'s is difficult. Newmann recommends that staff not focus on individual proficiency as a sole criterion; rather, they should try to retain a perspective on the total project. Newmann is opposed to giving grades but does feel an evaluation of students' work should involve completion of definite levels of work, giving private feedback to enhance learning, and ample documenting of student activities.

Role of the Teacher

The demands on teachers involved with citizen action are substantial. In general, teachers can adopt four different roles in a social action program. The most common role is as general resource, one who supplies information on people, places, and resources in the community, as well as on procedures and strategies. In the role of counselor, the teacher tries to respond to the needs of all students in all projects. The counselor role deals with emotional or psychophilosophic dilemmas rather than with information on community contacts or action strategies. In a third role, the teacher acts as an expert resource in a specific area (e.g., environment or racial self-determination). In this role the teacher becomes more closely involved with a specific project than in the previous two roles. Finally, there is the role of activist. Here the teacher aims to influence public policy and becomes actively involved in the project. Needless to say, each role has certain problems associated with it. It is important that teachers be comfortable and authentic with any role(s) they adopt.

Administration of the Program

A well-equipped citizen laboratory can contribute greatly to the program.

> Access to a variety of equipment: telephones, mimeograph and photocopy machines, cameras, tape recorders, equipment for making signs and posters, loudspeakers, filing cabinets, typewriters, televisions, radio. Materials such as stationery and stamps, mailing lists, specialized directories, maps, selected legal references, periodicals and newspapers should be available. Students also need rooms for small and large group meetings and space for storing project-related materials.[15]

Another administrative concern is liability. Newmann suggests that parents and students be fully informed as to possible risks associated with the instruction. After being informed about the program, parents and students should give written consent to participate in the course under the disclosed conditions. Finally, the teacher and other adults involved should take reasonable actions to prevent harm to students in the program.

A citizen advisory committee consisting of parents, students, teachers, and a few community leaders can also be established. The committee can help advise on general policy and contribute to program visibility and security.

A general principle of the program is the involvement of students in decision making. For example, students can take part in determining the program schedule, use of space equipment, and policy regarding visitors and public relations. A community meeting should hold a central place in the governing structure. All paid staff and students in the program would be voting members. These meetings would focus on communication of program information, decisions on program policy, and social activities. A possible governance structure is shown in figure 8.2.

SUMMARY AND APPRAISAL

This is an impressive model. Newmann has carefully developed a rationale for his action-oriented approach as he has thoughtfully examined the various conceptual issues—

Figure 8.2. A Governance Structure

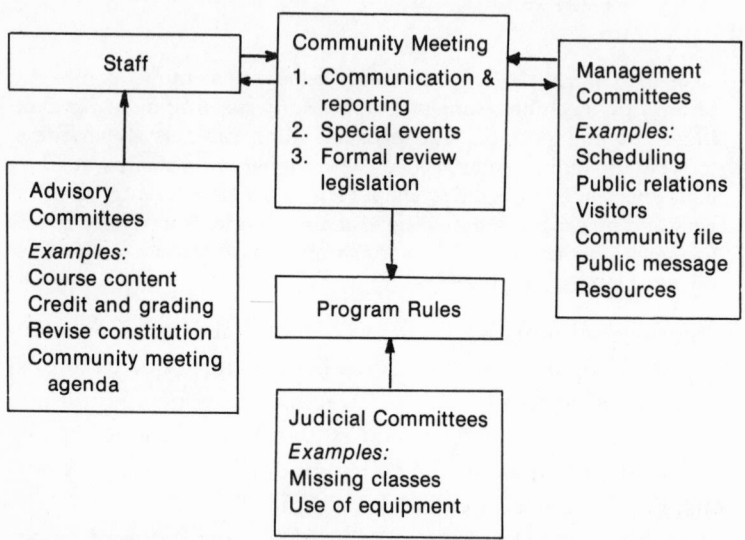

Source: Fred Newmann, Thomas Bertocci, and Ruthanne M. Landsness, *Skills in Citizen Action: An English–Social Studies Program for Secondary Schools* (Skokie, Ill.: National Textbook, 1977), p. 111.

psychological, philosophical, and moral—associated with the
model and provided persuasive reasons for its implementation.

In presenting the model he has also developed a comprehensive discussion of its components and has not avoided some of
the problems that relate to the approach. He acknowledges
the psychological issues as well as the administrative concerns
associated with the approach. This discussion also reveals some
genuine hindrances to the approach. For example, an extensive
lab must be made available for the courses in the program. In a
day of declining enrollments and increasing costs, it is unlikely
that some school boards would approve this expense. Another
potential problem is the "disruption" the course might cause in
the school. In some schools it is difficult for students to even
obtain hall passes, and the thought of letting students pursue

projects outside the school could be a major administrative problem. Such administrative "difficulties" can prevent implementation of new programs.

A related issue is the climate of the school in which the program is implemented. If the school does not provide a context for democratic participation by students and staff, it is somewhat incongruous to encourage participation in a larger social context.

Newmann's discussion of the curriculum and the classroom procedures is also somewhat general; there are few specific examples of the program in operation. Although the format (e.g., the courses) is outlined in detail, there are few specific examples of classroom activities (e.g., discussion procedures), and this could hinder program implementation. Someone initiating a social action program could benefit from classroom examples from Newmann's work in Madison, Wisconsin.

In spite of these problems, this program provides students with a way to actively participate in the democratic process. No other model presents a richer opportunity for this involvement.

REFERENCES

Principal Sources

Newmann, Fred. *Education for Citizen Action: Challenge for Secondary Curriculum*. Berkeley, Calif.: McCutchan, 1975.

In this book Newmann builds a strong case for a social action program at the secondary school level. There is emphasis on the rationale and context for such a program as well as a general description of a program in operation.

Newmann, Fred; Thomas A. Bertocci; and Ruthanne M. Landsness. *Skills in Citizen Action*. Skokie, Ill.: National Textbook, 1977.

The authors outline the citizen action program in more detail and describe how a program can be implemented in a school setting. Along with *Education for Citizen Action*, this book should provide enough information for a school staff interested in initiating such a program.

Related Readings

Jones, W. Ron. *Finding Community: A Guide to Community Research and Action*. Palo Alto, Calif.: James E. Freel, 1971.

National Commission on the Reform of Secondary Education. *The Reform of Secondary Education: A Report to the Public and the Profession.* New York: McGraw-Hill, 1972.

Report of the Panel on Youth of the President's Science Advisory Committee. *Youth: Transition to Adulthood.* Chicago: University of Chicago Press, 1974.

9
CARING, JUDGING, AND ACTING

Let's return to our original theme: the importance of caring, judging, and acting in the practice of morality. All six of the moral education models we have studied are concerned with these three realms, but each reveals this concern in a different way. In this final chapter we would like to show how a teacher might draw selectively on the strengths of each model in order to deal with morality's three facets.

CARING

One way to see caring is through the window of the heart. From this point of view, caring is a feeling of support for oneself and concern for others. The biblical injunction to "Love thy neighbor as thyself" is perhaps the most widely known expression of caring. Caring embodies the sentiment for humanity and the disposition of benevolence. As a feeling, caring stirs us to contribute to the goodness of people's lives.

Clearly, caring involves emotion. If we hated people, we

would feel no need to understand or aid them. But caring is more than a warm feeling or a humane spirit. It is also a quality of thinking and appraising. For the extent to which we are moved to care in a given situation depends largely on our capacity to understand the meaning of another's experience. For example, it is easy for us as adults to care about, or empathize with, the teen-ager who stomps away after failing to make a critical shot in a basketball game. Our understanding of the game and the importance of such activities to adolescents gives us a real sense of the youngster's feelings.[1] A young child could not care in this way—not because he is "bad" but because he would be unable to fathom the complexity of motivations, needs, and emotions at stake. Or, consider how difficult it often is for teachers and parents to care about the subtle pleasures and pains of a child's experiences in a sandbox, on a jungle gym, or during a game of marbles. An overall concern and love for the child will not in itself tune us in to the full meaning these activities hold for the child. We have to stretch our imaginations to appreciate the child's feelings. Of course, if love isn't there to begin with, we will not even bother to try to understand. The point is, caring recruits our emotions and our thoughts; we need both to want to understand people's needs and to know how to understand them.

How can teachers inspire the desire to care and promote the ability to understand in their students? The models that provide the best answers to this question are rationale building, consideration, and cognitive moral development.

In the rationale building model, Shaver discusses the importance of nurturing the motive to care in students. One way to do this, Shaver suggests, is by giving children practice in "caring" behaviors. Young children can be taught to listen attentively to their classmates' point of view, to do their share at clean-up time, and to wait their turn at lunch even before the principles of tolerance and mutuality are comprehended in abstract form. In other words, children can practice democratic behaviors while they are learning the rational justification for such behaviors. In trying out caring acts, such as helping a classmate solve an arithmetic problem, a child may see in a concrete way the value of caring. By consistently reinforcing and modeling caring behaviors, the teacher helps nourish the children's desire to care. Shaver stresses that the teacher must also strive to help students see the "why" behind specific practices. A child's question about the reason for rules like coming to school on time and not eating during spelling lessons should be greeted as a healthy sign of intellectual and moral development. A focus on caring behaviors thus needs to be followed up with discussions of the reasons for such behaviors. Nonetheless, one can ill afford to skip over the modeling of moral behaviors. Specific practice in democratic, or "caring," behaviors may pave the way toward a more general moral reflectiveness.

As Shaver suggests, teachers, especially teachers of young children, must at times explicitly model, or act-out, alternative solutions to social problems and provide direct instruction in strategies of interpersonal caring. As the psychologist and educator Thomas Lickona has written:

> A teacher can show children how to solve a social problem. In one study (Doland and Adelberg, 1967), an adult used puppets to act out alternative solutions to conflicts—fighting over and breaking a toy wagon, for example, as opposed to taking turns to the satisfaction of both parties. Preschoolers who watched these little dramas and discussed the various alternatives became less aggressive and more cooperative in their own play.
>
> Teachers can also directly suggest ways of dealing with a problem situation. To a child who is pushing another for a seat, the teacher can say, "You can ask Billy to move over." To a child who wants another's toy instead of the one he has, she can say: "You can ask Ben to trade with you." To a child who is trying to defend his claim to something: "Tell Peter, I'm playing with this now, you can have a turn later." To a child who is the victim of aggression: "You tell John in a loud voice, 'I don't like that! The rule is no hitting!' " [2]

In the sense in which Shaver and Lickona describe it, the judicious use of modeling or direct instruction can promote "caringness" among students.

A basic way in which teachers model moral behavior is through their actions toward their students. Outside the home, the teacher is probably the single most potent exemplar of morality in children's lives. The teacher has a special obligation to "practice what she preaches." That this consistency is not always achieved was brought home to one of the authors recently in an in-service workshop. In the course of the workshop (it concerned student behavior) the teacher-participants identified three major concerns about students in their school: lack of respect for teachers, vulgar language, and sloppy notebooks. As the workshop progressed, however, the teachers exhibited each of the behaviors for which they had criticized their students. The teachers did not listen to one another, thus conveying a lack of mutual respect; they used "vulgar language"; and their chart papers were often unreadable. While it is easier to teach morality than practice it, such hypocrisy must surely backfire in the long run.

The teacher's role as a moral model is crucial. But children learn to care not only by observing the teacher but through their experiences in the classroom environment as a whole. McPhail's consideration approach and Kohlberg's cognitive moral development model discuss at length environmental qualities that stimulate students to care about others.

The two models look at the development of caring from different angles. McPhail focuses on the emotional climate in the class and the "feeling" side of caring, whereas Kohlberg concentrates on the intellectual quality of the environment and the cognitive dimension of caring. McPhail argues that "as important as reason and logic may be in the process of educating, the desire to learn comes mostly from the feeling that we are cared for and cared about as persons." [3] The teacher must strive to create an atmosphere in which each student feels accepted and at home. Kohlberg, too, believes that an atmosphere of mutual trust is essential for the development of caring, but he would describe this atmosphere in more cognitive terms than does McPhail. According to cognitive developmental theory, a morally stimulating class environment is one that offers rich opportunities for role taking. Role taking means assuming the perspective of another. A class in which only one or two perspectives are provided or encouraged is an educationally impoverished one, Kohlberg argues. Children learn to care about other people by being challenged by different points of view. Without difference there is no challenge and hence no development. Kohlberg suggests that the child's need to make sense out of his or her social world impels caring about others. In this view, the child has an inherent need to try to balance conflicting perspectives—a need on which the teacher must capitalize. McPhail urges teachers to honor the child's need for love; Kohlberg directs our attention to the child's need to understand.

Whether the need to understand or the desire for love is the more compelling factor in psychological development is a fascinating theoretical question. But, on a practical level, it is clear that caring is promoted by a combination of intellectual and emotional factors. Students need sympathetic encouragement and intellectual challenge. How to make the child feel loved and challenged at the same time is a question that no one can answer definitively. The answer lies more in the art of teaching than in its science.

In any case, there is a great deal of similarity in the materials and activities built around the consideration and the cognitive moral development models. To be sure, Kohlberg's programs generally contain more probing questions and attend more explicitly to the "judging" dimension of morality. But the difference is predominantly one of emphasis, not substance. McPhail's "sensitivity cards" might, for example, present a situation in which a teen-age girl is stood up on an important date, or a boy's parents are worried about his backpacking trip and ask him to stay home. The students are then asked to imagine themselves in the stories' roles. An example of a situation, or a dilemma, in a cognitive developmental approach is the tree-climbing affair. In this lesson, students are asked to alternatively take the roles of Holly and her father, where Holly faces the decision whether to climb a tree to save a cat's life, although she has promised her father not to climb trees. In both McPhail's and Kohlberg's "situations," the goal is to induce students to walk in the shoes of other people.

McPhail's and Kohlberg's models are also complementary in their emphasis on the need to provide many and varied opportunities for children to cooperate in school—to work together toward common goals in pairs, small groups, or as a whole class. Such work helps children both feel and understand the need to take other viewpoints into account. The fruits of collective problem solving are evident in the responses of a group of kindergarten children whose teacher assigned many group projects. The children defined cooperation this way: "You help people do things; like if they can't make a 3, you show them how." "You gotta talk nice, or no one will listen to you." "You can't be too bossy—everyone has to have a turn." And, "It means to help with the work, you know, like don't goof off." [4]

The cognitive moral development model singles out one form of group problem solving as especially beneficial: the class meeting, which gives students an opportunity to collaborate with one another and the teacher in setting rules and resolving conflicts. The "just community" experiment in the Cambridge public schools is essentially a class meeting concept writ large. In a typical elementary school setting, the class meeting is held daily, or weekly, in a circle so that all may see one another. In one first-grade class, the children volunteered and agreed on the following rules for discussion: "Sit in the circle, raise your hand if you want to talk, listen to others when it is their turn, and sit outside the circle in a chair if you do not cooperate." [5] These first graders discussed at their meetings such issues as how best to organize clean-up details, what to do when other individuals in your group don't do their work, and how to express sympathy to a classmate in the hospital. In a just community high school, issues such as stealing, cutting classes, and neglect of homework may be raised, as well as the more positive concern of curriculum planning.

The subject of widening student roles in educational decision making leads us into the next domain of morality: judging. Class meetings surely compel students to make judgments among competing alternatives. Caring, however deeply, about a problem is not sufficient to solve it. Conscious and careful deliberation is required.

JUDGING

Moral judgments deal with questions of moral obligation and questions of moral value. We make judgments of moral obligation when we say that a certain action is morally right or wrong, or ought or ought not be done.[6] Examples of such judgments are "children ought to respect their teachers," "people should keep their promises," and "segregation in schools is morally wrong." When we talk about duty, or what is morally right or wrong, we are talking about how we should act toward one another. But right or wrong discourse is not the only way we use moral language. We often speak of a person as being "good" or "moral," for instance, without necessarily referring to a right or wrong action. When we make judgments about people, motives, or traits of character, as opposed to judgments about actions or practices, we are expressing our view of what is good or bad, worthy or unworthy, about people. We state what we *value*, rather than what we are *obligated* to do. Examples of judgments of moral value are "my sister is a good woman," "revenge is an ignoble motive," and "self-fulfillment is the only legitimate goal of education." Ultimately, statements of moral value are claims about what the good life consists of, what is fundamentally worthwhile, and what should be pursued, cherished, and passed on to the next generation.[7]

Because people have different and incompatible beliefs about what is "good," we have the concept of "right." Judgments of obligation, of what is right, are ways in which we seek to resolve conflicts in moral values. Since judgments of obligation try to establish what is fair among people, they are not personal in the same sense that judgments of value are personal. Whether or not Susan values personal pleasure, for example, has no direct bearing on the welfare of others. That she believes pleasure to be "a good" is not in and of itself a matter of justice or injustice. But if, one Saturday morning, Susan is valuing personal pleasure, which leads her to want to sleep late, and her mother is valuing industriousness and cleanliness, which leads her to ask that Susan clean the kitchen, a moral conflict can develop. For the question is no longer what Susan or her mother values, but what is the fairest way to work out the differences in their values. Fairness implies that we try to rise above narrow self-interest and adopt an impartial or objective perspective.

Many people feel uncomfortable with the whole notion of moral obligation. To these individuals, there seems little need to talk of "should" and "ought." In the counseling department of the university where two of the authors work, there is a sign that says *Don't Should On Me*. The point of the sign is well taken. Nobody wants to feel dominated by another's versions of the "right," or, for that matter, do we wish to be enslaved by our own inner voice of conscience. One can be "shoulded" to death—by parents, teachers, employers, spouses, or even by oneself. The goal of moral education is not to produce emotionally constricted individuals who torture themselves and others with questions of moral obligation. Yet, there is a tendency on the part of many to avoid such questions altogether—an avoidance that can be as driven as the obsessiveness of the moralizer. One of the author's friends, who incidentally is well balanced emotionally, saw the sign in the counseling department and remarked: "Yes, shoulds are an emotional waste." We would suggest, however, that in certain contexts "shoulds" are not only unavoidable but also extremely important.

Sissela Bok, in her book *Lying: Moral Choice in Public and Private Life*, poses a perplexing number of moral questions that have dramatic implications for human relations in medicine, law, politics, and the family. Just glancing at the first few pages of the book confronts the reader with a set of crucial "should" questions:

> Should physicians lie to dying patients so as to delay the fear and anxiety which the truth might bring them? Should professors exaggerate the excellence of their students on recommendations in order to give them a better chance in a tight job market? Should parents conceal from children the fact that they were adopted? Should government lawyers lie to Congressmen who might otherwise oppose a much needed welfare bill? And should journalists lie to those from whom they seek information in order to expose corruption? [8]

"Should" questions hold little promise of disappearing in the future. As we create more options for ourselves, and for our children, the complexity of the moral issues we face seems to increase. It would be nice to think that "should talk" is an unnecessary residue of Puritan rigidity, but that does not seem to be the case. For the challenge of moral decision making has intensified in the wake of Watergate, the Bakke decision, Karen Ann Quinlan's case, and the like.

But let's turn back to children and schools. Few children, or even adolescents, face in their own lives the kinds of questions Sissela Bok raises. Of course, one response to this assertion is to argue that if students are not exposed to these issues in their classes, and helped to sift through them intellectually, how will they be able to handle them effectively as adults? Apart from this future-directed rationale, there is the essential consideration that kids grapple with their own moral concerns—concerns that can form the basis for important class discussions and activities. Elementary school students, for example, invariably harbor questions about fairness in family and peer relations: Should household chores come before "fun time"? Who should get to decide what TV show to watch? Should I give a quarter to my friend for ice cream if his parents told him not to eat ice cream? Should I tell the teacher that my friend cheated on an arithmetic test? What should be done about the fist fights and pencil stabbings on the playground? Young children do wrestle with moral problems. Teachers can help children meet these problems on firmer ground.

The most extensive and focused materials that relate to children's moral conflicts can be found in Kohlberg's program. As an example of an effective lesson in the cognitive developmental tradition, consider the following excerpt from the School Rules Unit, part of a multidisciplinary program on rules and laws developed by the teachers and curriculum staff of the Tacoma public schools. Like most dilemmas, this one may be role-played, discussed, and responded to in writing.

That's Not Mine

Pat and Chris sit down at a table together in the cafeteria with their lunches. At Pat's place is a left-over peanut butter sandwich from the last lunch. Pat says, *"Yuk!"* and pushes the sandwich to Chris's place. Chris says, "That's not mine," and flips the sandwich back onto Pat's tray. The sandwich lands in Pat's mashed potatoes. Pat gets up and shoves Chris, knocking him off his stool. Chris bumps his nose on the table while falling and it starts to bleed. Chris gets up and hits Pat in the face, giving him a black eye. A circle of kids forms around the two of them. Students are yelling and pushing each other to see.

Comprehension questions:
1. How did the fight start? What was the argument about? What were Pat and Chris fighting about?
2. What did Pat do with the sandwich when he first sat down?
3. What was Chris's response?
4. Who got hurt?
5. What did the other students in the cafeteria do?

Role-taking questions:
1. Do you think Pat was angry when he pushed the sandwich? Why do you think so?
2. Do you think Chris was angry when he threw the sandwich back? Why do you think so?
3. If you were Chris, would you have thrown the sandwich back? Why or why not?
4. Does Pat think Chris meant to throw the sandwich into the mashed potatoes?
5. If you were Pat and the sandwich landed in your mashed potatoes, what would you do? Why?
6. Does Chris think Pat meant to hurt him by giving him a shove? Explain what you mean.

Decision-making questions:
1. What possible things could Pat do when the sandwich lands in his mashed potatoes besides shoving Chris? Which of these is the best thing to do and why?
2. After Chris is knocked down, what should he do? Why? What are all the different things which he might do (his alternatives)?

3. What would happen (the consequences) if he did each of these things?
4. What would be his best alternative?
5. Can you think of a rule which might have prevented this incident?
6. In some schools there is a rule that each person cleans up his/her own place after eating. Is there more than one rule that might apply here? What are they? (*Note:* Teachers might list on the board rules which the kids come up with.)
   a. Each person should clean up his/her own place after eating.
   b. Students should not throw food in the lunchroom.
   c. No fighting in the lunchroom.
   d. Students should stay in their seats during lunch.
   List these rules in their order of importance to you. The most important is number one. Which of these rules is the most fair? Which rule works best? Which rule is followed most? Why? [9]

In trying to create a productive discussion of dilemmas like "That's Not Mine," teachers often find that students aren't "ready" for a serious discussion. A seventh-grade teacher recently remarked to one of the authors: "With a lot of my kids, I feel it's a triumph for them to stop calling one another names, let alone engage in all that high-level role taking and debating." Discussion is certainly not an easy or a "natural" process. As we pointed out in our discussion of the just community (see chapter 7), teachers commonly need to model the communication skills a discussion demands. A film that shows students holding an open yet focused discussion may help kids see what a good discussion entails. A series of such films is available from the Far West Laboratory for Research and Development in Education, in their minicourse on leading controversial discussions. Tapes can be made of class discussions and played back for analysis to zero-in on a particular skill. Also, students may take turns acting as observers of class debates or problem-solving sessions. Finally, as one can see in Fred Newmann's social action model, entire minicourses can be devoted to developing the skills of political advocacy and persuasion. As students gain competency in the discussion method, the range and complexity of issues that may be introduced expands. As Israela Aron has written:

> Students with little experience in deliberation could be presented with relatively well-defined problems, involving a limited number of possible solutions, and accompanied by fairly complete information as to the consequences of each alternative. As the students become more and more practiced, the complexity of the problems could be increased: the problem could be stated vaguely and its definition contested, there could be a wide range of possible solutions, information on the consequences of proposed solutions might be scant or might require students to do some research. [10]

Not only is it helpful to begin with clearly defined and relatively straightforward issues, it may also be helpful to give students practice in carrying out specific functions in a discussion. For example, one student might try on the role of "summarizer," in which he brings ideas together so that the group can refocus on the problem. Another student might experiment with "initiator," which asks her to propose and define the task, or issue, for the group. Still another student might keep a watch on the emotional climate of the discussion and assume the role of "gatekeeper," in which he asks others to participate in the discussion and keeps the channels of communication open. The task of clarifying and mediating conflicts among group members and reducing the anxiety level might fall to the "harmonizer."

Of course, the nature of the roles depends to a large degree on the nature of the discussion. If the discussion is a problem-solving session that requires a consensus (e.g., the group has to come up with a single policy position on President Carter's proposed tax reforms), the skills of compromising, bargaining, and consensus testing (checking with the group to see whether they are reaching a decision) are crucial. In open discussions of moral dilemmas, however, agreement is not the goal, and harmonizing and consensus-testing roles are much less relevant. But several standard roles are common to both kinds of discussion: clarifier, summarizer, encourager, information provider, moderator, and standard setter. There are also common hindering moves in a discussion, for which students should be alert. Such moves include

1. *Seeking recognition:* calling attention to oneself through unusual behavior such as telling stories, boasting, and loud talking.
2. *Digressing:* getting away from the topic or the group task.
3. *Out of field:* withdrawing from the discussion.
4. *Blocking:* interfering with the group task by arguing excessively or by continually bringing up a "dead" issue.[11]

A set of guidelines and tasks for holding effective class meetings that we have found particularly useful is the following:

Roles for Student Involvement in Class Meetings

1. *Chairperson.* The role of the chairperson (this may be the teacher at the beginning of the year) is to call the meeting to order. Assign other roles or solicit volunteers for the other roles. Keep the meeting on task. See that the meeting runs in an orderly manner. Recognize speakers. Review and observe the rules of procedure. Probe the thinking of the speaker. Bring the meeting to a close. When deemed necessary, the chairperson has the right to make the procedural decision.
2. *Recorder.* The role of the recorder is to keep a log of the class meeting. List what to record and look for.
3. *Friend of the chair.* The role of the friend of the chair is to help the chair with procedural matters, especially as students begin to assume this role. The chairperson can consult with the friend of the chair on matters of procedure, etc., and the friend of the chair can suggest a possible decision for the chairperson.
4. *Agenda writer.* The role of the agenda writer would be to check the log book for unfinished topics and write those on the board. The agenda writer could also confer with the teacher to see if other topics should be listed. Topics

for the agenda can be suggested on the bulletin board. *Optional:* Students may assume this role when the teacher feels they are ready.

5. *Bulletin-board keeper.* The role of the bulletin board keeper is to remove completed issues from the bulletin board and keep the bulletin board in neat order. If there are no topics suggested on the bulletin board, the keeper of the board should attempt to generate interest among students in topics for discussion.

6. *Paraphraser.* The role of the paraphraser is to restate the points made by other students during the discussion. A student who seldom feels comfortable contributing to the class meeting can be asked to take the role of paraphraser.

7. *Summarizer.* The role of the summarizer is to restate the important conclusions or differing points of view at the end and/or during the meeting.

8. *Silencer.* The role of the silencer is to use a predetermined signal in getting the group to resume listening. *Examples:* hands behind ears, hand over mouth, turn off lights, hold up flag or sign.

9. *Speakers' order.* The role of the speakers' order is to record the names of the students who wish to speak on the board. Students should wait until a speaker is finished before raising their hands to have their name recorded.

10. *Teller.* The role of the teller is to hand out ballots for issues needing a secret ballot. The teller then counts the ballots and posts the results. The teller can also call the role and record the votes as yes, no, or present. Students could also use two or three colored marbles to vote on an issue. Another quick vote could be the use of red and green backed cards to vote. (Paste red construction and green construction paper on the two sides of 5 x 7-inch cards.)

11. *Dealer.* A student can be assigned to the role of poker chip dealer to help keep students on the topic. The dealer will have the task of passing out poker chips to the speakers as the meeting or discussion goes on. The

dealer gives a white chip to a student who speaks on any topic, a red chip to students who speak on a similar subject and a blue chip to those who kept to the topic. The dealer will collect the chips at the end of the meeting. *Note*: the teacher or chairperson can review the chips to determine (*a*) who spoke often, (*b*) who could not stay on the topic, and (*c*) who was able to sometimes stay on task but wandered off at times.[12]

In addition to distributing roles in the discussion, a further technique that many teachers find necessary is to incorporate a vocabulary lesson or two in the basic concepts of social, legal, and political relations. Many students are handicapped in discussion because they do not have the verbal knowledge to communicate their concerns. In order to get a discussion off the ground, a teacher may need to explain the difference between such concepts as fact and value, opinion and inference, or law and custom. Many students need help in defining words like *rule, role, authority, decision making, dilemma,* and *issue*. Of course, students don't have to use sophisticated philosophical or sociological categories to carry on a productive discussion. A teacher can in fact lead a fruitful inquiry-oriented discussion on the meaning of key concepts like "facts," and where they come from, or "inferences," and how they are distinguished from facts. These concepts can also be taught in an expository fashion, which is the more appropriate method if the teacher wants to move quickly to the moral heart of an issue. In other words, if students are familiar with the fundamental terms of moral discussion, they will spend more time analyzing alternative perspectives and less time asking for definitions or groping for words.

Just as individual concepts can be taught relatively directly to students, so, too, can a method for analyzing complex moral problems. Value analysis furnishes such a method. The model is similar to cognitive moral development in its emphasis on thorough deliberation but is more step-by-step in its articulation than is Kohlberg's strategy. Because value analysis concentrates on such skills as distinguishing fact from judgment, collecting and assessing facts, and predicting consequences, it enables students to break down the process of decision making into manageable parts. Value analysis is used extensively by secondary school social studies teachers, for it helps students deal effectively with moral decisions that hinge on the careful use of data and the rigorous assessment of consequences. Such issues as Should we continue to deregulate the airline industry? or Should we vote for the proposed nuclear power plant in our community? are well handled with the value analysis framework.

Because value analysis sets forth a tightly structured sequence of intellectual procedures, some teachers feel it is a bit sterile and artificial. In reference to an approach similar to value analysis, Aron has cautioned:

> The great temptation for educators following this approach would be to break up the process of deliberation into a number of smaller components and fashion out of them a series of mechanical exercises. The process of inquiry outlined by Dewey in *How We Think* has been treated in this fashion innumerable times, with uniformly disappointing results. This reductionist and disjointed strategy destroys the organic unity of the process of deliberation and makes deliberation abstract and academic. [13]

To be sure, solving a moral problem is not merely a matter of technical skill or intellectual dexterity. A computer, for instance, could never decide a moral question. No machine can determine whether someone should have an abortion, or whether someone should tell her child that she was adopted. Our moral judgments ultimately rest on our beliefs about the nature of human beings and the purpose of social life. The ways in which these beliefs influence our perceptions, thoughts, and feelings cannot be pinned down neatly in a formula or axiom. We cannot, in other words, "program" morality into students by teaching them a system or moral analysis. "Morality is made for man, not man for morality," William Frankena has written. Similarly, value analysis should not be internalized mechanically, as if in itself it represented moral goodness; it should be used creatively as a teaching aid.

In using value analysis in secondary school classrooms, we

have found it helpful to vary the sequence of activities. Rather than always beginning with identifying the value question and assembling purported facts, we sometimes skip to step 5, "arriving at a tentative value decision." In this case, we encourage students to solve the problem in a flash, based on their intuitive response, and then to write the response in a short paragraph. The paragraphs are put aside, and the students are asked to work through the value analysis process from step 1. Finally, they are requested to write a short essay comparing the intuitive and the analytic paths to problem solving. As a follow-up activity, a reading about "right-brained" versus "left-brained" decision making is assigned and discussed in class. Variations such as this help students not only master value analysis but also think critically about it.

Another model that deals with "judging" is values clarification. This approach concentrates on judgments of moral (and nonmoral) value, rather than on judgments of obligation. "Should" questions are not found in values clarification lessons. The focus is on what students believe to be "good." Nevertheless, judging does come into play because the model requires that values be chosen "freely, from alternatives, after thoughtful consideration of the consequences." For instance, a values clarification exercise might ask students to decide whether physical beauty, professional success, or close friendship is the most important value to them. The teacher would generally ask the students to think of reasons for their choice. The teacher's request for reasons is not intended to help students probe deeply or critically into their belief systems, or to take the perspective of other people. The teacher's role is less one of challenging students to think more carefully than it is one of encouraging them to express their feelings. Values clarification is thus most appropriately used to "loosen up" the class, to make kids feel at home when communicating their personal beliefs. More intellectually productive models, such as the cognitive moral development model and value analysis, can then be employed with greater ease and effect.

Acting

As teachers we like to think that what we do in the classroom has an impact on "life outside." If we teach our students to analyze values and reason morally, we hope that this will influence their behavior in the "real world." One way we can help students translate ideas into action is by according them a certain amount of decision-making responsibility in the classroom and school. Class meetings, student-directed grievance boards, and the like provide an opportunity for kids to put their moral beliefs to the test. While such practice is crucial, it is nonetheless not the same as "real world" decision making. For this reason, educators like Fred Newmann have developed programs to help young people deal with actual justice issues in the community. The social action model, as its name implies, not only views students as members of the community of the school but also as citizens of the community at large.

Newmann makes a strong case for integrating citizen action projects with moral reasoning and value analysis programs. For it is only through citizen action courses that students can gain the environmental competence necessary for meaningful moral discourse. Without the ability to influence one's society, Newmann stresses, an individual may not even address the question "What should I do?" If there are no real alternatives, Newmann asks, why should anyone engage in moral deliberation? If a student is powerless to affect moral outcomes, the weighing of interests and alternatives can seem completely irrelevant. Students must feel a measure of control over their environment in order for effective moral thinking to take place. Dilemmas like "Should Harry Truman have ordered the atom bomb dropped on Japan?" or "Should Bakke have been admitted to medical school?" may mean very little to students who see no hope of influencing public policy. But if the school can help the student exert an impact in the immediate community, an interest in larger social and political issues may develop.

Newmann's model contains six separate courses. They are devoted to the political-legal process, communications, community service internships, citizen action, action in literature, and public message. Obviously, administering and teaching a social action program is a complex undertaking. And, as we pointed out in chapter 8, Newmann discusses the frustrations and limitations of the program in an honest and straightforward manner. What is heartening is that Newmann provides a survival manual for those who want to set up community action programs. Armed with *Skills in Citizen Action*, a teacher might experiment with small-scale adaptations of Newmann's six-course program. Moral action projects, in one form or another, are well within the reach of most secondary school teachers.

In this book we have tried to show that moral education is as many-sided an endeavor as morality itself. The ideas and techniques of moral education speak to our emotional, rational, and active selves. They help us extend ourselves to others, to resolve or accept conflicts with others, and to realize our beliefs in action. Moral education is not one more subject to teach, something the class does every Thursday at 1:45. It is a commitment to explore with students in an ongoing way the moral significance of academic subjects and classroom events. Its goal is to make morality a living concern for students, to breathe moral life into the material they read and the relationships they form. Moral education does not deliver moral answers or prescribe moral practices. What it does is to cultivate the moral sensitivity and sharpen the moral reasoning of young people. Ultimately, it may help them create a more just society.

NOTES

Chapter 1. Issues in Moral Education

1. Jacob Bronowski, "A Moral for an Age of Plenty," *Saturday Evening Post*, 233, no. 20 (12 November 1960); reprinted in Bronowski, *A Sense of the Future*, ed. Piero Ariotti. (Cambridge, Mass.: MIT Press, 1977), pp. 202–5.
2. William K. Frankena, *Ethics* (Englewood Cliffs, N.J.: Prentice-Hall, 1973), p. 25.
3. Peter McPhail, J. R. Ungoed-Thomas, Hilary Chapman, *Learning to Care* (Niles, Ill.: Argus Communications, 1975), p. 30.
4. Ibid., p. 45.

Chapter 2. Historical Context for Moral Education

1. Edward Gray, July 4th Oration, delivered in Boston, 1790, Orations Collection, American Antiquarian Society, Worcester, Massachusetts.
2. George Burrill, July 4th Oration, delivered in Providence, 1797, American Antiquarian Society.
3. Thomas Sparhawk, July 4th Oration, Boston, 1798, American Antiquarian Society.
4. *The Boston Primer* (1808), cited in Stanley K. Schultz, *The Culture Factory, Boston Public Schools, 1789–1860* (New York: Oxford University Press, 1973), p. 17.
5. Carl Kaestle, *The Evolution of an Urban School System, New York City, 1750–1850* (Cambridge, Mass.: Harvard University Press, 1973), p. 113.
6. Ibid.
7. *A Manual of the System of Discipline and Instruction* (New York, 1850), pp. 19–20; cited in Kaestle, *Evolution of an Urban School System*, p. 116.
8. Ibid.
9. Kaestle, *Evolution of an Urban School System*, p. 117.
10. *Annual Report of the Rhode Island School Board, 1884*; cited in Charles Carroll, *Public Education in Rhode Island* (Providence, 1918), p. 204.
11. Kate Wiggin, *Children's Rights* (Boston: Houghton Mifflin, 1892); cited in Bernard Wishy, *The Child and the Republic* (Philadelphia: University of Pennsylvania Press, 1977), p. 125.
12. Ibid.
13. G. Stanley Hall, *Forum* 32 (1901–2): 24–25; cited in Lawrence Cremin, *The Transformation of the School* (New York: Vintage, 1964), p. 103.
14. Charles Strickland and Charles Burgess, eds., *Health, Growth and Heredity, G. Stanley Hall on Natural Education* (New York: Teachers College Press, 1965), p. 22.

15. G. Stanley Hall, "The Ideal School as Based on Child Study," in National Educational Association, *Addresses and Proceedings, 1901*, p. 475; cited in Strickland and Burgess, *Health, Growth, and Heredity*, p. 22.
16. Strickland and Burgess, *Health, Growth, and Heredity*, p. 24.
17. John Dewey, "Ethical Principles Underlying Education," in National Herbart Society, *Third Yearbook, 1897*; reprinted in Reginald Archambault, ed., *John Dewey on Education* (Chicago: University of Chicago Press, 1964), p. 129.
18. John Dewey, "The School and Society," in Archambault, *John Dewey on Education*, pp. 300–302.
19. Cremin, *The Transformation of the School*, p. 307.
20. Ibid., p. 333.
21. Ibid., pp. 325–26.
22. See, for example, Jules Henry, *Culture Against Man* (New York: Random House, 1963); Philip Jackson, *Life in Classrooms* (New York: Holt, Rinehart and Winston, 1968); Jonathan Kozol, *Death at an Early Age* (Boston: Houghton Mifflin, 1967); and John Holt, *How Children Fail* (New York: Pitman, 1965).
23. Jerome Bruner, "The Process of Education Revisited," *Phi Delta Kappan*, September 1971, p. 21.

Chapter 3. The Rationale Building Model

1. James Shaver and William Strong, *Facing Value Decisions: Rationale Building for Teachers* (Belmont, Calif.: Wadsworth, 1976).
2. Ibid., p. 15.
3. Thomas Green, *The Activities of Teaching* (New York: McGraw-Hill, 1971), p. 47.
4. Shaver and Strong, *Facing Value Decisions*, p. 22.
5. Ibid., p. 25.
6. Israel Scheffler, *The Language of Education* (Springfield, Ill.: Charles C Thomas, 1960), pp. 57–58.
7. Shaver and Strong, *Facing Value Decisions*, p. 93.
8. Ibid., pp. 101–2.
9. Ibid., pp. 112–13.
10. Ibid., p. 103.
11. Donald Oliver and James Shaver, *Teaching Public Issues in the High School* (Boston: Houghton Mifflin, 1966), p. 128.
12. Shaver and Strong, *Facing Value Decisions*, p. 104.
13. Oliver and Shaver, *Teaching Public Issues*, p. 129.
14. Ibid., p. 128.
15. Shaver and Strong, *Facing Value Decisions*, p. 22.
16. Ibid., p. 44.
17. Ibid., p. 25.
18. Ibid., p. 132.

Chapter 4. The Consideration Model

1. Peter McPhail, J. R. Ungoed-Thomas, and Hilary Chapman, *Learning to Care* (Niles, Ill.: Argus Communications, 1975). Unless otherwise cited, all quotes in this chapter are taken from this source.

2. Abraham Maslow, *Motivation and Personality* (New York: Harper & Row, 1970).

3. Peter McPhail, J. R. Ungoed-Thomas, and Hilary Chapman, *Sensitivity*, booklet from section 1 of the Lifeline program (Niles, Ill.: Argus Communications, 1975).

4. Peter McPhail, J. R. Ungoed-Thomas, and Hilary Chapman, *Consequences*, booklet from section 1 of the Lifeline program (Niles, Ill.: Argus Communications, 1975).

5. Peter McPhail, J. R. Ungoed-Thomas, and Hilary Chapman, *Points of View*, booklet from section 1 of the Lifeline program (Niles, Ill.: Argus Communications, 1975).

6. Peter McPhail, J. R. Ungoed-Thomas, and Hilary Chapman, *Rules and Individuals*, booklet from section 2 of the Lifeline program (Niles, Ill.: Argus Communications, 1975), p. 24.

7. Peter McPhail, J. R. Ungoed-Thomas, and Hilary Chapman, *Who Do You Think I Am?*, booklet from section 2 of the Lifeline program (Niles, Ill.: Argus Communications, 1975), pp. 25–26.

Chapter 5. A Valuing Process and Clarification Model

1. Louis E. Raths, Merrill Harmin, and Sidney Simon, *Values and Teaching* (Columbus, Ohio: Merrill, 1978).

2. Ibid., p. 10.

3. Howard Kirschenbaum, *Advanced Values Clarification* (La Jolla, Calif.: University Associates, 1977).

4. Raths et al., *Values and Teaching*, p. 26.

5. Ibid.

6. Ibid., pp. 27–28.

7. Ibid., p. 70.

8. Ibid., p. 69.

9. Ibid., p. 67.

10. Ibid., p. 71.

11. Ibid., pp. 68–69.

12. Ibid., p. 72.

13. Ibid., pp. 64–65.

14. Ibid., p. 55.

15. Ibid., p. 57.

16. Ibid., p. 101.

17. Sidney Simon, Leland Howe, and Howard Kirschenbaum, *Values Clarification* (New York: Hart, 1972).

18. Raths et al., *Values and Teaching*, pp. 128–37.

19. Simon, et al., *Values Clarification*, p. 39.

20. Ibid., pp. 59–60.

21. Ibid., p. 95.

22. Ibid., pp. 172–73.

23. Ibid., pp. 241–42.

24. Raths et al., *Values and Teaching*, p. 249.

25. Ibid., pp. 8–9.

26. Alan Lockwood, "A Critical View of Values Clarification," in *Moral Education: It Comes with the Territory*, ed. David Purpel and Kevin Ryan (Berkeley, Calif.: McCutchan, 1976), pp. 155–56.

27. Ibid., p. 167.
28. Ibid., p. 280.

Chapter 6. Value Analysis
1. Lawrence Metcalf, ed., *Values Education: Rationale, Strategies, and Procedures* (Washington, D.C., National Council for the Social Studies, 1971).
2. Jerrold Coombs, "Objectives of Value Analysis," in Metcalf, *Values Education*, p. 17.
3. Ibid., p. 15.
4. Ibid., pp. 16–17.
5. Ibid., p. 17.
6. Jerrold R. Coombs and Milton Meux, "Teaching Strategies for Value Analysis," in Metcalf, *Values Education*, p. 29; and Milton Meux, "Resolving Value Conflicts" in ibid., pp. 122–23.
7. Coombs and Meux, "Teaching Strategies for Value Analysis," p. 40.
8. Ibid., p. 46.
9. Ibid., p. 52.
10. Ibid., pp. 56–57.
11. Ibid., p. 55.
12. Ibid., p. 59.
13. Ibid., p. 60.
14. Milton Meux, "Resolving Value Conflicts," in Metcalf, *Values Education*, p. 122.
15. Ibid., pp. 129–30.
16. Ibid., p. 131.
17. Ibid.
18. Ibid., p. 144.
19. Ibid., p. 147.
20. Ibid.
21. Ibid., p. 163.
22. Ibid., p. 164.

Chapter 7. The Cognitive Moral Development Model
1. Lawrence Kohlberg, "The Adolescent as a Philosopher," *Daedalus*, Fall 1971, p. 1059.
2. Lawrence Kohlberg, "The Claim to Moral Adequacy of a Highest Stage of Moral Judgment," *Journal of Philosophy* 40 (1973): 639.
3. John Rawls, *A Theory of Justice* (Cambridge, Mass.: Harvard University Press, 1971).
4. Kohlberg, "The Claim to Moral Adequacy," p. 641.
5. Moshe Blatt and Lawrence Kohlberg, "The Effects of Classroom Moral Discussion on Children's Levels of Moral Judgment," *Journal of Moral Education* 4 (1975): 153.
6. This section is derived from Richard H. Hersh, Diana Pritchard Paolitto, and Joseph Reimer, *Promoting Moral Growth: From Piaget to Kohlberg* (New York: Longman, 1979), chap. 5.
7. Blatt and Kohlberg, "The Effects of Classroom Moral Discussion," p. 153.
8. This section is derived from Hersh, Paolitto, and Reimer, *Promoting Moral Growth*, chap. 7.

Chapter 8. The Social Action Model

1. Fred W. Newmann, *Education for Citizen Action: Challenge for Secondary Curriculum* (Berkeley, Calif.: McCutchan, 1975), pp. 4–5.
2. Ibid., p. 18.
3. Ibid., p. 29.
4. Ibid., p. 35.
5. Ibid., p. 47.
6. Ibid., pp. 54–55.
7. Ibid., p. 55.
8. Ibid., p. 91.
9. Fred Newmann, Thomas Bertocci, and Ruthanne M. Landsness, *Skills in Citizen Action: An English–Social Studies Program for Secondary Schools.* (Skokie, Ill.: National Textbook, 1977), pp. 9–10.
10. Ibid., p. 6.
11. Ibid., pp. 48–49.
12. Ibid., p. 10.
13. Ibid.
14. Newmann, *Education for Citizen Action*, p. 143.
15. Ibid., p. 126.

Chapter 9. Caring, Judging, and Acting

1. Suzanne Smither, "A Reconsideration of the Developmental Study of Empathy," *Human Development* 20 (1977): 256.
2. Thomas Lickona, "Creating the Just Community with Children," *Theory into Practice* 16, no. 2 (April 1977): 103.
3. Peter McPhail, *Learning to Care* (Niles, Ill.: Argus Communications, 1975), p. 9.
4. Judi Kur, "Love Is Working Together," *Mini-Book*, Project Change, vol. 5, no. 1 (Cortland, N.Y.: State University of New York, April 1977), p.6.
5. Ruth Giese, "Responsibility: the 4th 'R'," *Mini-Book*, p. 21.
6. William Frankena, *Ethics* (Englewood Cliffs, N.J.: Prentice-Hall, 1973), p. 9.
7. Dwight Boyd, "The Moralberry Pie: Some Basic Concepts," *Theory into Practice* 16, no. 2 (April 1977): 69.
8. Sissela Bok, *Lying: Moral Choice in Public and Private Life* (New York: Pantheon, 1978), pp. xv–xvi.
9. Tacoma Public Schools, *The Ethical Quest in a Democratic Society* (funded by the National Endowment for the Humanities, School Rules Unit, 1978), p. 26.
10. Israela Ettenberg Aron, "Moral Philosophy and Moral Education: A Critique of Kohlberg's Theory," *School Review* 85, no. 2 (February 1977): 527.
11. K. R. Benne and P. Sheats, "Functional Roles of Group Members," *Journal of Social Issues* 4, no. 2 (1948).
12. Tacoma Public Schools, *Ethical Quest*, p. 21.
13. Aron, "Moral Philosophy and Moral Education," p. 528.

INDEX